GRAMMAR IN PRACTICE

Sentences and Paragraphs

Lesli J. Favor, Ph.D.

AMSCO SCHOOL PUBLICATIONS, INC.
315 HUDSON STREET, NEW YORK, N.Y. 10013

Cover Design: Meghan J. Shupe
Cover Art: picturequest.com/Thinkstock
Text Design: Nesbitt Graphics, Inc.
Compositor: Nesbitt Graphics, Inc.

When ordering this book, please specify: *either* **R 019 W** *or*
GRAMMAR IN PRACTICE: SENTENCES AND PARAGRAPHS

Please visit our Web site at: ***www.amscopub.com***

ISBN 978-1-56765-135-5
NYC Item 56765-135-4

2 3 4 5 6 7 8 9 10   10 09 08 07 06

About the Author

Lesli J. Favor loves grammar! She began her career in education as a writing tutor at the University of Texas at Arlington. After earning her BA in English there, she earned her MA and Ph.D. at the University of North Texas. While there, she taught courses in composition and literature. Afterward, she was assistant professor of English at Sul Ross State University-Rio Grande College. Now, as an educational writer, she is the author of fourteen books for young adult readers and students. She lives in the Seattle area with her husband, two dogs, and a horse.

Consultants

Nancy Mae Antrim is an assistant professor of English and Linguistics at Sul State University. Her Ph.D. is in linguistics from the University of Southern California. Prior to completing her doctorate, she taught ESL at Riverside High School in El Paso, Texas. Currently her teaching and research interests involve language teaching and methodology and second language acquisition. She has presented her research at numerous national and international conferences.

Belinda Manard has served as K–12 English Curriculum Specialist for Canton City Schools in Ohio for the past nine years. In this role, she develops and tests curriculum and assessments aligned with the state's ELA standards and provides staff development for teachers. Previously, she taught English for nineteen years at McKinley Senior High School in Canton, serving as department chair as well as the school's test coordinator. She holds a BS in English, Communications, and Theater from Miami University of Ohio and a M.Ed. from the College of Mount St. Joseph.

Gary Pankiewicz has been teaching high school English for ten years at Hasbrouck Heights High School in Bergen County, New Jersey. He received his BA and MA (with a concentration in Composition Studies) from Montclair State University.

for Kathryn Rogers,
grammar goddess

Contents

INTRODUCTION
How to Use This Book
—and Why

A thorough understanding of grammar and the mechanics of writing is one of the pillars of a solid education. It prepares you for success in college, careers, and daily life. For this reason, now more than ever, students are being asked to demonstrate proficiency in grammar, usage, and composition. State tests, the SAT, and the ACT will measure your ability to recognize and correct errors in grammar and mechanics. These tests, along with classroom assignments, require that you write clear, correct sentences and paragraphs, both in isolation and in essay format.

This book is the last in a three-book series that offers instruction, review, and practice in the basics of grammar, mechanics, and composition. The concepts build on one another, from the parts of speech through paragraph composition, so that by the end of the series, you will have the tools necessary to assemble polished compositions. The first book, *Grammar in Practice: A Foundation*, covered the parts of speech, grammar rules, punctuation, capitalization, and spelling. The next book, *Grammar in Practice: Usage*, offered expanded instruction on grammar, common usage errors, and using different kinds of sentences. In this book we will show you how to pull together your grammar and usage skills to write strong, engaging sentences and paragraphs.

In this book you will find a variety of lessons, features, and activities that will challenge you to think and to write:

- **Instructional sections:** Short, easy to read sections introduce and explain key concepts, complete with definitions, explanations, and examples. Your teacher may skip sections you already know well and return for review to sections that were especially helpful or important.

- **Activities:** Workbook-style exercises let you practice applying lesson concepts. Some exercises require you to read and respond to a given passage or analyze specific points of mechanics or style in an excerpt.

- **Composition Hints:** These features offer tips and techniques for applying rules and for developing your personal style in writing.

- **Writing Applications:** To help you integrate the writing concepts you learn, you'll often be asked to write and revise sentences and paragraphs, occasionally working with a classmate. Writing prompts throughout the book offer many opportunities for practice.

- **Research Applications:** These assignments at the end of each lesson group ask you to research one of several topics and write about it. Practicing the skills of sentence and paragraph writing while you explore a topic that interests you will let you showcase your strengths while incorporating your individual style and creativity. Many of the topics focus on technology.

- **Test Practice:** Each lesson group concludes with a practice test covering only the material in those lessons. Additionally, the book concludes with a comprehensive test covering the major concepts. The tests are usually multiple choice and are modeled after state-proficiency and standardized tests you will take in order to graduate or apply to colleges.

With so much variety, this book is an invaluable classroom tool. Your teacher can pick and choose lessons, work in order from beginning to end, or have you use the book as a resource when you write essays. However you and your teacher decide to use it, you will learn to craft sentences and paragraphs that are more varied, precise, clear, and sophisticated. Use the entire series and you will be able to write interesting and effective compositions with confidence and flair.

Lesli J. Favor, Ph.D.
Author

Auditi Chakravarty
Editor

1 Sentence Composition

All written communication begins with the sentence. In every writer's quest to express ideas, opinions, and other thoughts, he or she struggles to write clear, forceful sentences. Writers may compose sentences only to realize they are monotonous or lacking in style and variety.

When such challenges face you, don't give up! The lessons in Part One show you how to write strong, engaging sentences. For starters, Lesson 1 coaches you in the composition of the four sentence types. You will practice not only writing each type but also combining sentences to create stronger, more pleasing sentences.

Lessons 2 and 3 show you what qualities make clear, forceful, engaging sentences. In the activities, you'll practice writing sentences that are concise, clear and specific, unified, forceful, and varied in length and structure. Finally, in Lesson 4, you'll review and reinforce everything you've learned.

With these lessons and with a little practice, you can compose sentences that say what you mean in a fresh and effective way.

The Four Sentence Types

The four sentence types are *simple, compound, complex,* and *compound-complex.* Each type is built from one or more *clauses.* In this lesson, we will first examine clauses, and then we will turn our attention to sentence types.

Every complete sentence has at least one main clause (sometimes called an independent clause).

 A *main clause* contains a subject and its verb and expresses a complete idea. It can stand alone as a sentence.

In the following examples, the subject is underlined <u>once</u>, and the verb is underlined <u>twice</u>.

MAIN CLAUSES: American <u>folklore</u> <u>includes</u> stories, songs, dances, and more.

Many <u>characters</u> in folklore stories <u>are</u> fictional.

<u>Others</u> <u>are based</u> on real-life people, such as Daniel Boone.

Besides a main clause, some sentences contain one or more subordinate clauses (sometimes called dependent clauses).

 A *subordinate clause* contains a subject and its verb but does not express a complete idea. It cannot stand alone as a sentence.

The word *subordinate* means "occupying a lower position." We use *subordinate* to label clauses that are in a lower position than, or *dependent* upon, a main clause. Specifically, the subordinate clause depends on the main clause to complete the expression of thought.

In the examples below, notice that each subordinate clause expresses an incomplete thought. Because the thought is incomplete, these clauses cannot stand alone as a sentence. We call them sentence *fragments.* In particular, the word that begins each clause raises an idea that is left incomplete. Below, these words are *when, because,* and *which.*

SUBORDINATE CLAUSES: when Daniel Boone blazed the Wilderness Trail

(The clause has a subject, *Daniel Boone,* and a verb, *blazed.* But the idea of "when" is incomplete. What happened or was true *when* Boone blazed the trail?)

because pioneers needed a path through Cumberland Gap

(The clause has a subject, *pioneers,* and a verb, *needed.* But what happened or was true *because* pioneers needed the path? The thought is incomplete.)

which was a settlement in Kentucky territory

(The clause has a subject, *which,* and a verb, *was.* But what noun or pronoun is this clause saying was a settlement? The thought is incomplete.)

To form a complete sentence, a subordinate clause must be joined to a main clause. In the following examples, each main clause is underlined once, and each subordinate clause is underlined twice.

SENTENCES: <u>When Daniel Boone blazed the Wilderness Trail</u>, <u>the Kentucky wilderness opened up</u>.

(Now the thought is complete. We know what happened when Boone blazed the trail.)

<u>Boone created the trail</u> <u>because pioneers needed a path through Cumberland Gap</u>.

(Now the thought is complete. We know what happened because pioneers needed a path.)

<u>Boone founded Boonesborough</u>, <u>which was a settlement in Kentucky territory</u>.

(Now the thought is complete. We know that Boonesborough was a settlement.)

ACTIVITY 1

On the line provided, label each item *main* for *main clause* or *sub.* for *subordinate clause*. If the item is a main clause, insert a capital letter and a period to show that it can stand alone as a complete sentence.

Samples:

__main__ **a.** A̲nother folkloric legend was Calamity Jane.

__sub__ **b.** whose real name was Martha Jane Canary

_____ **1.** she dressed like a man in pants and hat

_____ **2.** who was one of the Pony Express riders

_____ **3.** which were written about the exploits of Calamity Jane

_____ **4.** when Sam Bass stole cattle and robbed trains

_____ **5.** which was the stuff of legends

_____ **6.** according to legend, he buried gold in secret caves

_____ **7.** although no one has ever found the gold

_____ **8.** ballads tell of Sam Bass's outlaw adventures

_____ **9.** most Americans have heard of Johnny Appleseed

_____ **10.** since he planted apple orchards for four decades

A main clause that stands alone as a sentence is called a *simple sentence.* Look at your work in Activity 1. Each item you marked correctly as *main* is a simple sentence.

By joining main and subordinate clauses in various ways, we construct the other three sentence types. Study the following definitions and examples of all four types. In the examples, each subject is underlined once, and each verb is underlined twice.

SENTENCE TYPE AND DEFINITION	EXAMPLES
A *simple sentence* contains one main clause and no subordinate clauses. *Note: The subject, the verb, or both can be compound.*	Billy the Kid gained fame as a gunfighter. At age 21, he died from a gunshot by Sheriff Pat Garrett. Jim Bowie and Davy Crockett defended the Alamo. Black Caesar escaped slavery and became a pirate. Black Caesar and Blackbeard met and then worked together.
A *compound sentence* contains two or more main clauses and no subordinate clauses. *Note: Main clauses can be joined by a comma and a connecting word or by a semicolon.*	Our folklore features Anglo characters, **but** it also includes American Indian characters. Bowie and Crockett were Anglos, **but** Pocahontas and Sitting Bull were Indians. Pocahontas helped the Jamestown settlers; Sitting Bull defeated General Custer at Little Bighorn.
A *complex sentence* has one main clause and at least one subordinate clause. *Note: At right, subordinate clauses are italicized. Words such as* although, that, *and* who *introduce subordinate clauses.*	*Although some of their exploits are true,* others have been enhanced. Ballads and stories exaggerate things *that happened*. People *who have become "larger than life"* are legendary.
A *compound-complex sentence* has at least two main clauses and at least one subordinate clause. *Note: In the examples, the words* that, what, *and* whether *introduce subordinate clauses.*	Paul Revere warned colonists *that the British were coming*, **and** he became the hero in a poem by Longfellow. Numerous folktales tell *what Davy Crockett did or said*, **and** he often seems superhuman. Billy the Kid supposedly killed twenty-one men by age twenty-one, **but** who really knows *whether this is factual*?

QUESTION: How can a knowledge of sentence types help me become a better writer?

ANSWER: You can become a better writer by starting with the simple sentence, the building block of all sentences. Even though it has only one subject and one verb, the simple sentence does not have to be simplistic. In fact, it can be just as powerful as the other, more complicated, types.

QUESTION: Okay. How can I write "powerful" simple sentences?

ANSWER: Your choices as a writer can transform a blah, basic simple sentence into a simple sentence that packs a punch. For example, you can combine related sentences into one improved simple sentence. The revision may have a compound subject, a compound verb, or both. By combining elements, you create a simple sentence that is effective, informative, sophisticated, and pleasing to read—powerful!

Read these two simple sentences:

John Frémont explored America's far West.

Jim Bridger, too, explored new territory in the West.

QUESTION: These sentences are grammatically correct. Why revise them?

ANSWER: Powerful sentences are not merely grammatically correct. They also engage readers by presenting ideas effectively. The two sentences above are technically correct, but they are repetitive in structure, which can turn off readers. One revised simple sentence presents the same information more effectively, as follows:

John Frémont and Jim Bridger explored new territory in America's far West.

The revised sentence has a compound subject, and it expresses all key ideas from the original sentences.

Study these additional examples.

ORIGINALS: Frémont surveyed the upper Mississippi and Missouri rivers.

He also mapped these waterways.

REVISION: Frémont surveyed and mapped the upper Mississippi and Missouri rivers.

(The sentences have been combined by using a compound verb.)

ORIGINALS: Jim Bridger and Kit Carson scouted for paths through the wilderness.

They guided expeditions along these paths.

REVISION: Jim Bridger and Kit Carson scouted for paths and guided expeditions through the wilderness.

(This revision has a compound subject and a compound verb.)

ACTIVITY 2

Each of the following items consists of two sentences. Combine each pair into one simple sentence with a compound subject, a compound verb, or both. (Make necessary changes to capitalization, punctuation, and subject-verb agreement.)

1. Buffalo Bill is an American folk hero.

Annie Oakley, too, is an American folk hero.

_____

_____

2. Buffalo Bill founded Cody, Wyoming.

He also created the Wild West Show.

_____

_____

3. As a teenager, Annie Oakley competed against Frank Butler, a sharpshooter.

She won the competition.

_____

_____

4. Frank lost the contest.

He won Annie's heart.

_____

_____

5. Annie and Frank got married.

They later joined the Wild West Show.

_____

_____

Eventually, using only simple sentences gets monotonous. The compound sentence adds variety to your writing, and it also serves another need: It allows you to join main clauses that express related ideas. Usually, we join the clauses with a comma and a conjunction such as *and, but,* or *nor,* or with a semicolon.

MAIN CLAUSE:	<u>Jim Bridger</u> <u>described</u> the Western territory to easterners.
MAIN CLAUSE:	<u>Many</u> of his tales <u>were</u> overly imaginative.
COMPOUND SENTENCE:	<u>Jim Bridger</u> <u>described</u> the Western territory to easterners, **but** <u>many</u> of his tales <u>were</u> overly imaginative.

(The revised version has two main clauses, each with its own subject and verb. The sentence is compound.)

ACTIVITY 3

Combine each pair of simple sentences to form one compound sentence. To do so, make changes directly to the printed sentences by crossing out periods and letters or words and writing corrections above them. Use a comma and *and, but,* or *or* to join the simple sentences, or use a semicolon.

> **Samples:**
>
> **a.** In Oklahoma, Myra Belle Shirley led horse thieves and cattle rustlers~~.~~;
> ~~she~~
> ~~Myra Belle Shirley~~ became the legendary Belle Starr.
>   but she
> **b.** Betsy Ross inspired folk stories too~~.~~, ~~This woman~~ was not a criminal.

1. Betsy Ross was a seamstress. She sewed the first "Stars and Stripes" American flag, according to legend.

2. In fact, Betsy Ross did make flags for the government. Historians can't verify the "Stars and Stripes" tale as absolute fact.

3. This first flag was made in 1776. The story about Ross's involvement did not emerge until 1870.

4. William Canby, Ross's grandson, told the story. Other Ross descendants backed him up.

5. Ross's house at 239 Arch Street in Philadelphia still stands. It is honored as the birthplace of the U.S. flag.

 Writing Application   Using Simple and Compound Sentences

What person from recent history do you think could become part of America's (or another nation's) folklore in the future? Think of someone whom the public sees as larger than life, someone whose actions, words, or accomplishments have been, or might one day be, exaggerated. A few possibilities are Elvis, Michael Jordan, Tiger Woods, Bill Gates, and Madonna.

On separate paper, write a paragraph of at least **five** sentences explaining who you think could be a folkloric character and why (in other words, how might he or she be seen as larger than life?). For each sentence, locate each clause and underline its subject once and its verb twice. Then label the sentence *simple* or *compound.* (Use at least two compound sentences.)

QUESTION: How can I use subordinate clauses to make my writing stronger?

ANSWER: With the subordinate clause, you can add another level of sophistication and specificity to your writing. (*Specificity* means "the quality of being specific.") Subordinate clauses help you express the specific relationships between ideas in complex and compound-complex sentences. Look at the following example.

MAIN CLAUSE: The <u>article</u> <u>included</u> a photograph of all students.

SUBORDINATE CLAUSE: who <u>won</u> ribbons at the science fair.

COMPLEX SENTENCE: The <u>article</u> <u>included</u> a photograph of all students *who <u>won</u> ribbons at the science fair.*

(The subordinate clause specifies exactly who is in the photograph. This detail is essential to the meaning of the sentence, but it is not the *main* idea. It strengthens the sentence by adding detail about the main idea.)

QUESTION: How do I write a subordinate clause?

ANSWER: A subordinate clause has a subject and a verb, but the clause is introduced by a word that makes the clause subordinate to, or dependent on, a main clause. Here are some of the words that introduce subordinate clauses.

Words That Introduce Subordinate Clauses

Noun clauses often begin with . . .	how, that, what, whatever, when, where, whether, which, whichever, who, whoever, whom, whomever, whose, why
Adjective clauses begin with relative pronouns, which are . . .	who, whom, whose, which, that
Adverb clauses begin with subordinating conjunctions, which include . . .	after, although, as, because, before, if, since, so that, than, unless, until, when, where, whether, while

Composition Hint

Often (but not always) a subordinate clause beginning with *that* is essential, while a subordinate clause beginning with *which* is nonessential.

ESSENTIAL: The folktale ***that*** *you told to the class* was riveting.

(This subordinate clause is essential, so it is *not* set off by commas.)

NONESSENTIAL: This folktale**,** ***which*** *I myself wrote*, is inspired by true events.

(This subordinate clause is nonessential, so it *is* set off by commas.)

Write a subordinate clause to complete each sentence below. Use the word in parentheses to introduce the subordinate clause. Be sure to add a period at the end of the sentence, if needed.

> **Samples:**
>
> **a.** *(until)* Enrique knew nothing about Wild Bill Hickock <u>until he read this folktale.</u>
>
> **b.** *(While)* <u>While her students completed a worksheet</u> , the teacher graded quizzes.

1. *(who)* I invited Jonathon, _____

2. *(because)* You should read this story _____

3. *(If)* _____ , you are breaking the law.

4. *(how)* The student did not know _____

5. *(Whoever)* _____ will pass the test.

Look at the sentences you wrote in Activity 4. Each of them is a complex sentence because it has one main clause and one subordinate clause.

Now take a quick look at the commas in the sentences you wrote in Activity 4. Normally, when a subordinate clause begins a sentence, a comma separates it from the main clause (see item 3). An exception is a sentence in which the subordinate clause serves as the subject of the sentence (see item 5). When a subordinate clause follows the main clause and is essential, a comma is not used (see items 2 and 4). A nonessential subordinate clause following a main clause is set off by a comma (see item 1).

Of course, a complex sentence can have more than one subordinate clause. Recall this complex sentence from Sample a:

Enrique knew nothing about Wild Bill Hickock *until he read this folktale.*

To add even more specificity, we can add another subordinate clause to the sentence.

Enrique knew nothing about Wild Bill Hickock *until he read this folktale <u>that tells about his exploits</u>.*

Composition Hint

Beware of adding too many subordinate clauses to a sentence. In some cases, it is better to break a sentence into two than have a long series of *that* or *which* clauses.

AWKWARD: Enrique knew nothing about Wild Bill Hickock until he read this folktale that tells about his exploits that occur in the rough, wild region that is known as the Wild West.

(Even though all the subordinate clauses help develop the main idea, the series of *that* clauses becomes awkward as it strings on and on.)

BETTER: Enrique knew nothing about Wild Bill Hickock until he read this folktale that tells about his exploits. The adventures occur in the rough, wild region that is known as the Wild West.

(The ideas are expressed in two well-formed, manageable complex sentences. Breaking the original sentence into two gives readers a chance to catch their breath.)

Add information to each complex sentence you wrote in Activity 4. To do so, add one more subordinate clause. Choose a word from the table on page 8 to introduce each new clause, and write each complex sentence on the lines below.

> **Samples:**
>
> *(The sample sentences below are revisions of the sample sentences in Activity 4.)*
>
> **a.** Enrique knew nothing about Wild Bill Hickock, who was a frontier marshal, until he read this folktale.
>
> **b.** While her students completed a worksheet, the teacher graded quizzes that they had just taken.

1. _____

_____

2. _____

_____

3. _____

_____

4. _____

_____

5. _____

_____

For each item, use the given clause to write a complex sentence. If you are given a subordinate clause, add a main clause to it. If you are given a main clause, add a subordinate clause to it. Make slight changes in wording, if desired, and write the complex sentence on the lines provided.

Hint: Review the information about using commas with subordinate clauses, which follows Activity 4 on page 9.

> **Samples:**
>
> **a.** when I read about Old West horse thieves
>
> *When I read about Old West horse thieves, I think of modern-day car thieves.*
>
> **b.** they are criminals
>
> *They are both criminals, although horse thieves seem more sensational.*

1. some people are famous for actions

_____

_____

2. who has become a legend

_____

_____

3. I wasn't interested in history

_____

_____

4. when you do a search on the Internet

_____

_____

5. people have not changed much

_____

_____

Composition Hint

Don't make your reader guess at the relationship between ideas in your sentences. Instead, use *subordinating conjunctions* to show the relationship. Notice the different meanings that can come from one pair of simple sentences, depending on how they are combined.

ORIGINAL: James Brady wore lots of diamond jewelry.

He was called Diamond Jim.

REVISED: **Because** James Brady wore lots of diamond jewelry, he was called Diamond Jim. (shows cause and effect)

REVISED: **Whenever** James Brady wore lots of diamond jewelry, he was called Diamond Jim. (shows time)

REVISED: James Brady wore lots of diamond jewelry **before** he was called Diamond Jim. (shows sequence)

The following table lists common subordinating conjunctions and tells what kind of relationships they show in sentences.

Subordinating Conjunctions and the Relationships They Show

after	shows that one action follows another action *Please go to the bank **after** you eat lunch.*
although	makes a contrast ***Although** the line at the bank was long, it moved quickly.*
as	shows that one action occurs while or when another action does ***As** I stepped up to the bank teller, the clock struck five o'clock.*
because	shows the cause, or reason, something happened or is true *I can get cash out of this machine **because** I have an ATM card.*
before	shows that an action occurs in advance of another action ***Before** I went to the bank, I stopped at the post office.*
if	expresses a condition *I would be grateful **if** you could lend me twenty dollars.*
since	shows the cause, or reason, something happens or is true; shows a sequence of time ***Since** I just got my paycheck, I can loan you the money.* (shows cause) ***Since** I started this job, I have had plenty of cash.* (shows time)
so	shows why something occurs or should occur; shows a consequence or reason *Sign the back of the check **so** the teller can cash it for you.* (shows why) *The bank was closed, **so** I withdrew cash from an ATM.* (shows consequence)
than	makes a comparison *Bianca saved more money in a month **than** I saved in a year.*
unless	expresses a condition *Spend less than you earn **unless** you want to go broke.*
when	shows that an action occurred at or during the time that something else happened or was true ***When** I was at the bank, I saw Paulo.*
where	expresses location *Show me **where** to sit, please.*
whether	expresses one or more options *I don't care **whether** you pay with cash or a credit card.*
while	shows that an action occurs during the time that something else happens or is true ***While** Gopal did homework, I balanced my checkbook.*

ACTIVITY 7

Write two different revisions for each of the following pairs of simple sentences. In each revision, use a different subordinating conjunction to form a complex sentence, and circle the conjunction.

> **Sample:**
>
> Jesse James became an outlaw.
>
> He used a false name, Thomas Howard.
>
> **a.** (When) Jesse James became an outlaw, he used a false name, Thomas Howard.
>
> **b.** Jesse James used a false name, Thomas Howard, (after) he became an outlaw.

1. He performed daring robberies.

Songs and ballads described his bravery.

a. _____

_____

b. _____

_____

2. James robbed banks.

He gave money to the poor.

a. _____

_____

b. _____

_____

3. James shared money with the needy.

He was a folk hero.

a. _____

_____

b. _____

_____

QUESTION: The compound-complex sentence seems complicated. How can I learn to write this sentence type?

ANSWER: This type may sound complicated, but don't despair. Like any other sentence, it is built from clauses. Specifically, you need at least two main clauses and at least one subordinate clause. Review the sample sentences in the chart on page 4. In addition, study the following example:

MAIN CLAUSE: Amelia Bloomer lived in the 1800s.

MAIN CLAUSE: She daringly wore loose "women's trousers."

SUBORDINATE CLAUSE: *when most women wore only dresses*

COMPOUND-COMPLEX SENTENCE: Amelia Bloomer lived in the 1800s *when most women wore only dresses*, **but** she daringly wore loose "women's trousers."

Since the compound-complex sentence contains several clauses, many writers focus first on writing a few related clauses. Then they combine the clauses to form a compound-complex sentence. At other times, writers notice that a compound sentence needs more detail, so they add a subordinate clause to provide the information. The result is a compound-complex sentence.

COMPOUND SENTENCE: Bloomer published a magazine, **and** in it she defended women's right to wear trousers.

(Readers may wonder what kind of magazine it was. The sentence would be stronger if it had a subordinate clause that provides this detail.)

SUBORDINATE CLAUSE: *that focused on women's rights*

COMPOUND-COMPLEX SENTENCE: Bloomer published a magazine *that focused on women's rights*, **and** in it she defended women's right to wear trousers.

Likewise, a writer may decide that a complex sentence needs another main idea expressed in a main clause. Adding the clause creates a compound-complex sentence.

COMPLEX SENTENCE: Bloomer became known for the garment, *which was jokingly called "bloomers."*

(This sentence is strong, but it could be more specific. Did Bloomer *create* "bloomers"? An additional main clause can provide the missing fact.)

MAIN CLAUSE: Bloomer had not invented women's trousers.

COMPOUND-COMPLEX SENTENCE: Bloomer had not invented women's trousers, **but** she became known for the garment, *which was jokingly called "bloomers."*

Revise each compound sentence to be a compound-complex sentence. To do so, insert a subordinate clause that you create. First, draw a caret (∧) where you want the subordinate clause to be inserted. Then write the subordinate clause above the caret. Use words from the table on page 8 to introduce the subordinate clauses.

Samples:

a. The assignment is an oral report, and it is due next week. *after the class visits the library*

b. Shamil will research Jesse James, and Arturo will research the Old West. *who was a bank and train robber,*

1. The library downtown has a great reference section, and it has some books.

2. You can use bound materials, or you can use microfilm and microfiche.

3. A librarian can help, but he or she should not do the hard work for you.

4. Students can access the card catalog online at home, or they can use the library's computers.

5. Consult various resources and list them in the bibliography.

Composition Hint

When you write a compound-complex sentence, make sure that you truly need a sentence with two main clauses and one subordinate clause (or more). Each clause in the sentence should succinctly express an idea that is clearly tied to the other clauses in the sentence. If you can write a less complex sentence that says the same thing, opt for the simpler, less wordy version.

In the examples below, each subordinate clause is in italics.

WORDY: Ahman was shocked to read the winning essay, for it was identical to the one *that he had written*.

(This compound-complex sentence has two main clauses and one subordinate clause. However, the information added by the subordinate clause could easily be expressed using just a few words instead.)

SUCCINCT: Ahman was shocked to read the winning essay, for it was identical to his own.

(This sentence is a compound sentence. The information did not justify a compound-complex sentence.)

SUCCINCT: Ahman presented proof *that someone had plagiarized his essay*, and the contest director retracted the offender's award.

(This compound-complex sentence is valid since none of the clauses can be reduced to just a few words without losing their meaning.)

In this book, you can turn to the section on conciseness in Lesson 2 (pages 17 and 18) to learn more about eliminating unnecessary words and phrases in sentences.

Writing Compound-Complex Sentences

Write your name at the top of a sheet of paper. On the paper, write a **complex** sentence about a topic that interests you. (Remember, a complex sentence has one main clause and one or more subordinate clauses.) With your teacher's approval, pass the sentence to the person sitting behind you.

Revise your classmate's sentence to be a **compound-complex** sentence. To do so, add a main clause to the complex sentence. Write the revised sentence underneath the original sentence. Underneath that, write a new **complex** sentence on a topic of your choice. Pass the paper to the person behind you.

Repeat this process one more time, so that you have written three sentences and revised three sentences. Retrieve the paper with your name on it and examine the sentences that have been written. Has each complex sentence been revised to be a compound-complex sentence? If one or both of the revisions are not compound-complex, revise them so that they are.

2 Clear, Forceful Sentences

Sentences vary widely in style and subject matter, yet all good sentences are clear and forceful. Compare the following two sentences:

WEAK: The city of Hollywood, which is in the highly populated state of California, is seen as the very focal point of the film industry in the country.

FORCEFUL: Hollywood, California, is the heart of America's film industry.

QUESTION: Why is the first sentence considered weak? After all, it uses a sophisticated sentence structure (it is a complex sentence).

ANSWER: The first sentence is weak due to wordiness and lack of unity, among other faults. It is true that a complex sentence structure is sophisticated, but only if every word contributes to the meaning of the sentence. In this example, though, many words are merely padding. When they are cut out, the revised sentence expresses the same idea succinctly.

QUESTION: Does this mean that I should try *not* to use complex and compound-complex sentences?

ANSWER: Absolutely not! Use a variety of sentence structures to express ideas that link tightly together, to make your sentences varied and vivid, and to add sophistication to your writing style. What's important is that every word count, whether the sentence is simple, compound, complex, or compound-complex.

QUESTION: What qualities make the second sentence clear and forceful?

ANSWER: It has several strong characteristics: *conciseness, clarity* and *specificity, unity,* and *active voice.* In this lesson, we examine each of these qualities in detail, and you will practice incorporating each quality into your own sentences.

Conciseness

Conciseness in writing means expressing yourself as simply and directly as possible. Never make a thought more complicated than it really is. To make your writing concise, avoid these five common errors.

1. Useless Words

Eliminate all useless words.

WORDY: Most movie previews make use of a film ratings system.

CONCISE: Most movie previews use a film ratings system.

               (Eliminate *make* and *of.*)

WORDY: These ratings are for the purpose of specifying a film's suitability for young viewers.

CONCISE: These ratings specify a film's suitability for young viewers.

               (Eliminate *are for the purpose of* and change *specifying* to *specify.*)

Here are a few other expressions that contain useless words, along with concise revisions:

WORDY	CONCISE
at a later date	later
for the purpose of	for
on a daily basis	daily

2. Duplication

Avoid saying the same thing twice, even in different words.

WORDY: Parents can refer back to a film's rating when deciding the question as to whether a movie is suitable for their kids.

CONCISE: Parents can refer to a film's rating when deciding whether a movie is suitable for their kids.

(Eliminate *back* and *the question as to*.)

Here are additional expressions that contain duplication, along with concise revisions:

WORDY	CONCISE
basic essentials	basics *or* essentials
cancel out	cancel
continue on	continue
a distance of five feet	five feet
each and every	each *or* every
end results	results
few in number	few
first began	began
future plans	plans
large/small in size	large/small
mail out	mail
past experience	experience
personal opinion	opinion
pleased and delighted	pleased *or* delighted
rarely ever	rarely
red in color	red
reduce down	reduce
repeat again	repeat
subject matter	subject
summarize briefly	summarize
in the month of June	June
until such time as	until

3. Wordy Construction

Do not use too many words to express an idea. The result is writing that sounds padded, pretentious, rambling, or "flabby." To eliminate wordiness, whenever possible condense a phrase to a word, and a clause to a phrase or even a word. Be a *which* hunter and eliminate every unnecessary *which* or *that*. Make every word in your sentence count.

WORDY: In the households of many, teens under the age of seventeen may not watch R-rated movies due to the fact that they contain violent images and profane language.

CONCISE: In many households, teens under seventeen may not watch R-rated movies because they contain violence and profanity.

    (Change *the households of many* to *many households*. Change *the age of seventeen* to *seventeen*. Change *due to the fact that* to *because*. Change *violent images* to *violence*. Change *profane language* to *profanity*.)

WORDY: The rating of G, which means General, designates a movie as being suitable for general audiences that include children.

CONCISE: The G, or General, rating designates a movie as suitable for general audiences.

    (Change the prepositional phrase *of G* to the adjective *G*. Change the clause *which means General* to the phrase *or General*. Eliminate the clause *that include children* since *general audiences* implies all ages.)

Here are commonly used wordy expressions, along with concise revisions:

WORDY	CONCISE
a number of	some
at the present time	now
at this point in time	now
despite the fact that	although
due to the fact that	because *or* since
during the time that	while
for the reason that	since *or* because
give consideration to	consider
hold a meeting	meet
in a timely manner	promptly *or* on time
in the event that	if
in the near future	soon
it is my understanding	I understand
limited number of	few
make preparations for	prepare for
on the grounds that	because

Revise the following sentences to make them more concise. Eliminate useless words, duplication, and wordy constructions. Write your new sentences on the lines provided.

> **Samples:**
>
> **a.** We held a meeting for the purpose of choosing films for the film festival.
>
> _____We met to choose films for the film festival._____
>
> **b.** Each person who is on the committee submitted a list of five films for consideration.
>
> ___Each committee member submitted a list of five films for consideration.___

1. We have held this film festival on a yearly basis since 2001.

   _____

   _____

2. From past experience, I knew that Laetitia would suggest movies that are romantic.

   _____

   _____

3. All films must meet requirements which are just a few in number.

   _____

   _____

4. For example, due to the fact that teenagers will attend the festival, all of the films that we show must have a PG-13 rating or lower.

   _____

   _____

5. Fairly often, we frequently meet on weekends to watch movies that have been proposed.

   _____

   _____

6. At a later time, we vote on which films to show.

   _____

   _____

7. After that has happened, our committee chair makes the decision, which is final, at a later date.

   _____

   _____

8. Usually we try to show films that represent a mix and variety of subject matter.

_____

_____

9. During the month of July, we show a different film each evening.

_____

_____

10. The cost of admission is one dollar, and we collect in about fifty dollars on a daily basis.

_____

_____

4. Elaborate Language

Learning and using challenging vocabulary is a valid goal, whether you do so for school, for work, or for personal enrichment. When you use these complex or elaborate words, be sure their use fits the needs of your audience. For example, in business settings, _compensation_ and _methodology_ name business actions or practices precisely. However, to tell your grandmother you got a raise in _compensation_ at your job sounds out of place. Similarly, _equitable_ and _witnessed_ are valid word choices for legal settings, but to say your curfew is not _equitable_ sounds unnatural, even silly.

In most cases, the elaborate or complex word choice is formal, even official sounding. Use complex words to make your writing as clear, specific, and appropriate as possible to your audience. The simpler word choice is informal or casual. Often—but not always—you'll use simple, direct words in your personal life and more complex words for school or business. In any case, choose the word that best fits your audience and the purpose of your writing.

ELABORATE: Please render your remuneration at the door.

SIMPLE: Please pay at the door.

ELABORATE: Is everyone cognizant that refreshments will be served pursuant to the movie?

SIMPLE: Does everyone know that snacks will be served after the movie?

Study this list of elaborate words and their simpler alternatives:

ELABORATE	SIMPLE
appreciable	many, much
assistance	help
cognizant	aware
commence	begin
compensation	pay
correspondence	letter(s)

ELABORATE	SIMPLE
disseminate	issue, send
endeavor	try
equitable	fair
expedite	rush, hurry
facilitate	help, ease
heretofore	until now
implement	do, carry out, follow
locality	place
methodology	method, way
modification	change
optimum	best, greatest, most
parameters	limits
preclude	prevent
procure	get, buy
purchase	buy
recapitulate	summarize
subsequent	later, next
terminate	end, stop
transmit	send
transpire	happen
utilize	use
witnessed	saw

5. Piled-up Modifiers

Avoid piling adjective upon adjective or adverb upon adverb. Where possible, use specific nouns and verbs to reduce the number of modifiers.

WORDY: Everyone loves a funny, delightful movie in the comedy category, such as one of Jim Carrey's many numerous films.

CONCISE: Everyone loves a comedy, such as one of Jim Carrey's many films.

(The noun *comedy* is more concise than the adjective-packed phrase *funny, delightful movie in the comedy category*. Also, *many numerous* is redundant; one of these adjectives is sufficient.)

WORDY: In *Liar Liar,* Carrey's character tries really really hard to deal with his sudden and unexpected inability to tell a lie.

CONCISE: In *Liar Liar,* Carrey's character struggles with his sudden inability to tell a lie.

(The verb *struggles* is more concise than the adverb-packed phrase *tries really really hard to deal*. Also, *sudden and unexpected* is redundant; *sudden* is sufficient.)

Revise the following sentences to make them concise, direct, and simple to understand. To do so, eliminate elaborate language and piled-up modifiers. (Use a dictionary if you need to.) Write your new sentences on the lines provided.

Samples:

a. The optimum environmental conditions in which to view a Jim Carrey film is with a little, young kid who is still youthful.

The best way to watch a Jim Carrey film is with a kid.

b. A young person's uninhibited, spontaneous nature allows him to chortle freely at every single one of the humorous, comical jokes.

A kid's open nature allows him to laugh at every joke.

1. Walk in a hurry over here to the place where I live so we can sit down together and watch _Bruce Almighty._

_____

_____

2. I have been eagerly looking forward to procuring my very own personal copy of this movie.

_____

_____

3. In _The Majestic,_ after a vehicular accident, Carrey's character walks uncertainly and tentatively into a small locality.

_____

_____

4. Due to amnesia, he is not cognizant or even very certain of who he is.

_____

_____

5. Of all Carrey's cinematic film works, perhaps the most popular and well liked is _Eternal Sunshine of the Spotless Mind._

_____

_____

Clarity and Specificity

Writing concisely is important, but a concise sentence that uses inexact or vague words is still weak. To make your writing as clear as possible, avoid these three common errors.

1. Inaccurate Connectives

Use the connective that expresses your thought accurately. Connectives include coordinating conjunctions, printed in italics below:

1. Use *and* to join sentences that express equal thoughts.

2. Use *but* or *yet* to join sentences that contrast with each other.

3. Use *or* or *nor* to join sentences that express two or more possibilities.

4. Use *for* to join sentences that express a cause and effect.

Connectives also include subordinating conjunctions such as *after, while, because,* and *if.* Take a moment to review "Subordinating Conjunctions and the Relationships They Show" on page 12.

CONFUSING: In 2004, Keisha Castle-Hughes was nominated for an Oscar, and the award went to Charlize Theron.

CLEAR: In 2004, Keisha Castle-Hughes was nominated for an Oscar, but the award went to Charlize Theron.

CONFUSING: Although Keisha was just thirteen years old, her nomination for a best actress award was especially impressive.

CLEAR: Because Keisha was just thirteen years old, her nomination for a best actress award was especially impressive.

QUESTION: Does it matter which conjunction I use to join simple sentences?

ANSWER: Yes, it matters. Different conjunctions have different purposes, as explained below.

1. Use *and* to join sentences that express equal thoughts.

Mandy worked the crossword puzzle, **and** Julian read the comics.

2. Use *but* or *yet* to join sentences that contrast with each other.

Mandy enjoys brain teasers, **but** Julian does not.

The puzzle was difficult, **yet** Mandy could easily finish it.

3. Use *or* or *nor* to join sentences that express two or more possibilities.

Did Julian build this model ship, **or** did Jim build it?

Jim is not interested in ships, **nor** did he build this model.

4. Use *for* to join sentences that express a cause and effect.

Julian worked carefully, **for** he wanted the model to be perfect.

2. The Inexact Word

Choose the word that expresses your thought accurately.

CONFUSING: Please find out if Keisha Castle-Hughes doesn't have an official Web site.

CLEAR: Please find out if Keisha Castle-Hughes has an official Web site.

CONFUSING: Don't fail to miss Keisha's portrayal of Pai in *Whale Rider.*

CLEAR: Don't miss Keisha's portrayal of Pai in *Whale Rider.*

CLEAR: Don't fail to see Keisha's portrayal of Pai in *Whale Rider.*

3. Vague, General Words

To add clarity and forcefulness to your writing, use words that express the specific meaning you have in mind.

VAGUE: People spoke well of the movie.

SPECIFIC: Critics praised *Whale Rider*.

VAGUE: People will enjoy learning about the native people of another country.

SPECIFIC: American viewers will enjoy learning about the Maori of New Zealand.

ACTIVITY 3

Revise each sentence to make its meaning clear and specific. Keep in mind the three preceding suggestions. Write your new sentences on the lines provided.

Samples:

a. You could apply for the job as ticket taker, but you could apply to work at the concessions counter.

   You could apply for the job as ticket taker, or you could apply to work at the concessions counter.

b. Grounds for dismissal from the job include honesty and tardiness.

   Grounds for dismissal from the job include dishonesty and tardiness.

1. Amber wanted to watch a Lindsay Lohan movie, and Viggo preferred one starring Johnny Depp.

_____

_____

2. Sonia could care less about horror movies.

_____

_____

3. I got hungry during the movie, when I went to buy popcorn.

_____

_____

4. The movie ended, and everyone stood and clapped.

_____

_____

5. Although Javier has a DVD player, we rented a DVD, not a videotape.

_____

_____

Replace each italicized word or phrase in the sentences with a more specific word or phrase from the list below. Write your choice on the line below the word or phrase it should replace. Use each choice only once.

Thanksgiving	grilled	basketball player
~~inform~~	hustled	splashed
prohibits	history class	~~scribbled~~
~~furious~~	Buena Vista Mall	Cedar Lake
hamburgers	basketball	tank tops and shorts
Brandon Jamison	King Senior High	American Eagle Outfitters

Sample:

a. Tanya ~~quickly wrote~~ a note to ~~tell~~ me she was ~~very upset~~ with me.
       scribbled   inform   furious

1. At *the lake,* we *cooked* some *food* and *went* in the water.

   _____

2. *The school* now *has a rule against* wearing *revealing clothing.*

   _____

3. *One of the stores* in *the mall* is hiring.

   _____

4. A *student* in my *class* hosted a *holiday* party.

   _____

5. The *athlete* caught the *ball* and *went quickly* down the court.

   _____

Unity

Follow these guidelines to create unity in a sentence.

1. Be sure that every part of a sentence is related to one main idea

Correct a lack of unity by breaking a sentence into shorter sentences or by subordinating one part of a sentence to a main part. (To review subordinate clauses and the words that introduce them, turn to page 8 in Lesson 1.)

LACKS UNITY: Live animals in movies are not harmed during filming, and many live horses were filmed in *Seabiscuit.*

               (Even though both clauses mention animals, the clauses have very different main ideas. One focuses on live animals in general, and the other focuses on horses.)

HAS UNITY:	Live animals in movies are not harmed during filming. Many live horses were filmed in *Seabiscuit*.
	(Each clause now forms a separate simple sentence. In the first, the main idea is the safety of animals during filming. In the second, the main idea is the filming of horses in *Seabiscuit*. The ideas are relevant to each other, but each requires a separate sentence.)
LACKS UNITY:	Horse racing is one theme in the movie, but the most important message is that underdogs can win.
	(The first clause is about horse racing. The next clause breaks the unity of the sentence by switching the focus to underdogs.)
HAS UNITY:	The most important message in the movie, which is about horse racing, is that underdogs can win.
	(The main idea of the entire sentence is the message about underdogs. The idea about horse racing is set in a subordinate clause beginning with *which,* making it clear that it is a secondary, not main, idea.)
LACKS UNITY:	Seabiscuit was a racehorse in the late 1930s, and Red Pollard, a former boxer, was the horse's jockey (rider).
	(The first clause tells about Seabiscuit, a racehorse. A clause joined to this one should express an idea closely linked to this main idea. However, the second clause tells who Red Pollard was. As a result, the emphasis moves from Seabiscuit to Red, breaking the unity of the sentence.)
HAS UNITY:	Seabiscuit was a racehorse in the late 1930s. Red Pollard, a former boxer, was the horse's jockey (rider).
	(The first sentence is unified around the subject of Seabiscuit, and the second sentence is unified around Red Pollard.)
HAS UNITY:	Seabiscuit was a racehorse in the late 1930s, ridden by jockey Red Pollard.
	(The entire sentence focuses on one main idea: Seabiscuit. The detail about Red is part of a phrase modifying *Seabiscuit,* so the focus stays on Seabiscuit rather than shifting to a new main idea.)
LACKS UNITY:	Seabiscuit gained fame in 1938, and he became Horse of the Year.
	(The two main ideas have no clear connection. The first clause tells when Seabiscuit gained fame, but what is the connection to the second clause, which tells about an award?)
HAS UNITY:	Seabiscuit gained fame in 1938 when he became Horse of the Year.
	(By subordinating the clause about the award to the first clause with *when,* the relationship between ideas becomes clear and unified. Now we know how the ideas are closely connected: The award led to Seabiscuit's fame.)

2. Avoid a series of *that*, *which*, or *who* clauses

Too many clauses make a sentence long and stringy, or cumbersome. To correct an unwieldy sentence, break it into shorter sentences or eliminate words to make the sentence more concise.

UNWIELDY:	The 2003 movie about Seabiscuit starred Tobey Maguire, who played the jockey, who was hired by Charles Howard, who was the horse's owner, who also hired the trainer, Tom Smith.
MANAGEABLE:	The 2003 movie about Seabiscuit starred Tobey Maguire, who played the jockey. The horse's owner, Charles Howard, hired him and the trainer, Tom Smith.
UNWIELDY:	The movie grew out of the book *Seabiscuit,* which was written by Laura Hillenbrand, who published this nonfiction novel in 2001.
MANAGEABLE:	The movie grew out of the book *Seabiscuit.* Laura Hillenbrand wrote this nonfiction novel, which was published in 2001.
MANAGEABLE:	The movie grew out of the nonfiction novel *Seabiscuit,* written by Laura Hillenbrand and published in 2001.

3. Use parallel structure

Make sure items in the sentence are parallel. Ordinarily, *and* and *but* connect like grammatical elements—for example, two or more nouns, verbs, adjectives, phrases, or clauses. Equal (like) grammatical elements are considered *parallel.*

NOT PARALLEL:	The movie is <u>suspenseful</u>, <u>entertaining</u>, and <u>it inspires</u>.
	(*Suspenseful* and *entertaining* are adjectives, but *it inspires* is a clause.)
PARALLEL:	The movie is <u>suspenseful</u>, <u>entertaining</u>, and <u>inspiring</u>.
	(The series includes three adjectives and is therefore parallel in structure.)
NOT PARALLEL:	Seabiscuit <u>was small</u>, <u>had knobby knees</u>, and <u>his front legs were crooked</u>.
	(*Was small* and *had knobby knees* each follow the structure of verb plus complement or object. However, *his front legs were crooked* follows a different structure: subject plus verb plus complement.)
PARALLEL:	Seabiscuit <u>was small</u>, <u>had knobby knees</u>, and <u>had crooked front legs</u>.
	(Now, all elements in the list follow that verb-first pattern, achieving parallel structure.)
NOT PARALLEL:	The jockey is <u>short and thin</u> yet <u>has strength</u> and <u>is capable</u>.
	(*Short* and *thin* is a pair of adjectives. The conjunction *yet* connects this pair to *has strength* and *is capable,* which begin with verbs. The two sets are not parallel.)
PARALLEL:	The jockey is <u>short</u> and <u>thin</u> yet <u>strong</u> and <u>capable</u>.
	(All four items are adjectives.)
NOT PARALLEL:	They practiced <u>on the track</u>, <u>racing along a dirt road</u>, and <u>in a field</u>.
	(The first and third items are prepositional phrases, but the middle item is a participial phrase.)
PARALLEL:	They practiced <u>on the track</u>, <u>on a dirt road</u>, and <u>in a field</u>.
	(All three items are prepositional phrases.)

Revise each of the following sentences. Write the revised sentence on the lines provided.

> **Samples:**
>
> **a.** Back in 1981, John Wilson began watching movies, evaluating them, and the ones that were the worst.
>
> Back in 1981, John Wilson began watching movies, evaluating them, and identifying the worst ones.
>
> **b.** He established the Razzie Awards, and they recognize the year's worst film, actors, and actresses.
>
> He established the Razzie Awards, which recognize the year's worst film, actors, and actresses.

1. Each year, awards are showered upon films, actors, actresses, and those who direct.

2. The Academy Awards show is televised nationally, and Billy Crystal makes an excellent host.

3. Billy Crystal has acted, done voice-overs, and he has performed comedy routines.

4. The Sundance Film Festival, which is a highly respected festival that honors independent films, which are not made by the big studios, occurs each year in Park City, which is in Utah.

5. Sundance award winners include *My Flesh and Blood, Genghis Blues,* and *American Dream*, but not all Sundance winners are available on DVD.

6. Another major award festival is the Independent Spirit Awards, which honor independent films, which include foreign films, which usually are not in English.

7. In 2000, Reese Witherspoon and Matthew Broderick starred in *Election,* but this film won an Independent Spirit Award.

_____

_____

8. When you like to choose films from themed lists, you will appreciate the American Film Institute's lists.

_____

_____

9. They group the top 100 films in various categories, and the Top 100 Thrills and the Top 100 Passions are two categories.

_____

_____

10. The 1942 film *Casablanca*, which stars Humphrey Bogart and Ingrid Bergman, who play star-crossed lovers, is a favorite of many who prefer older movies, which are known as classics today.

_____

_____

Active and Passive Voice

Often, you can make a sentence more forceful by writing the verb in *active voice* instead of *passive voice.*

PASSIVE VOICE: The movie was given five stars by Roger Ebert. (less forceful)

ACTIVE VOICE: Roger Ebert gave the movie five stars. (more forceful)

The *voice* of a sentence identifies the relationship between the subject and the verb.

 In an *active voice* sentence, the subject performs the action of the verb.

ACTIVE VOICE: Roger Ebert reviewed *Shakespeare in Love.*

Gwyneth Paltrow plays the role of Viola De Lesseps.

The film delighted audiences.

In the examples above, each subject is **active** in relation to its verb. Roger Ebert *reviewed.* Gwyneth Paltrow *plays.* The film *delighted.* The ideas in each sentence move forward from subject to verb to object. Each word is a power word because it is vital to the meaning of the sentence.

 In a *passive voice* sentence, the subject is acted upon; it receives the action of the verb.

PASSIVE VOICE: *Shakespeare in Love* was reviewed by Roger Ebert.

The role of Viola De Lesseps is played by Gwyneth Paltrow.

Audiences were delighted by the film.

In the previous examples, each subject is **passive** in relation to its verb. In other words, some other agent performs action *upon* the subject, and the subject just rests there and takes it in. *Shakespeare in Love* <u>*was reviewed*</u>. The role *is played*. Audiences *were delighted*.

QUESTION: How can I tell if a verb is in the passive voice?

ANSWER: The passive voice is formed by combining a form of the "to be" verb with the past participle of the main verb. (The "to be" verbs are *am, is, are, was, were, be, being, been*.) Here are examples of passive voice sentences:

SUBJECT	"TO BE" VERB	MAIN VERB	
Joseph Fiennes	is	featured.	*(What featured?)*
The movie	was	enjoyed.	*(Who enjoyed?)*
Paltrow	had been	interviewed.	*(Who interviewed?)*
Tickets	will be	purchased.	*(Who will purchase?)*

The passive voice sentences above do not identify who performs the action of the verb. When passive voice sentences contain this information, it usually takes the form of a prepositional phrase following the verb.

SUBJECT	"TO BE" VERB	MAIN VERB	PREPOSITIONAL PHRASE
Joseph Fiennes	is	featured	by the movie.
The movie	was	enjoyed	by viewers.
Paltrow	had been	interviewed	by David Letterman.
Tickets	will be	purchased	by many.

Even though the above sentences tell who performed the action, the sentences are still passive. Why? The verb is still in the passive voice. Now look at these sentences revised to be in active voice:

SUBJECT	VERB	DIRECT OBJECT
The movie	features	Joseph Fiennes.
Viewers	enjoyed	the movie.
David Letterman	had interviewed	Paltrow.
Many	will purchase	tickets.

In the active voice, we do not need a prepositional phrase to identify the doer of the action. The active voice sentences are more direct, more concise, more forceful.

ACTIVITY 6

In each sentence, identify the voice of the verb as *active* or *passive*, and write the appropriate label on the line provided. To help you get started, the verbs in the first five sentences are underlined.

Samples:

passive **a.** My admiration has been earned by actress Julia Stiles.

active **b.** She has starred in many enjoyable movies.

_____ 1. In *The Prince & Me,* a motorcycle <u>is ridden</u> by Paige Morgan.

_____ 2. Premed college classes <u>are taken</u> by her.

_____ 3. One day, she <u>meets</u> Eddie.

_____ 4. This role <u>is played</u> skillfully by Luke Mably.

_____ 5. The Paige character, by the way, <u>was brought</u> to life by Julia Stiles.

_____ 6. Paige enjoys activities with Eddie.

_____ 7. After a while, a secret about Eddie is learned.

_____ 8. Eddie is actually a Danish prince.

_____ 9. At first, Paige is angered.

_____ 10. But, of course, she later accepts Eddie's role in life.

QUESTION: How can I revise a sentence in the passive voice to be in the active voice?

ANSWER: First, find the verb. Then ask yourself who or what is performing the action of the verb. Usually, this "who" or "what" is a noun or pronoun following the passive voice verb. Finally, rewrite the sentence using this noun or pronoun as the subject.

EXAMPLE 1

Shakespeare is inspired by Viola.

STEP 1: What is the verb? It is *is inspired.*

STEP 2: Who is performing the action of inspiring someone? *Viola* is.

STEP 3: In active voice, the sentence is *Viola inspires Shakespeare.*

EXAMPLE 2

Shakespeare is portrayed by Joseph Fiennes.

STEP 1: What is the verb? It is *is portrayed.*

STEP 2: Who is performing the action of portraying? *Joseph Fiennes* is.

STEP 3: In active voice, the sentence is *Joseph Fiennes portrays Shakespeare.*

EXAMPLE 3

The film was reviewed by him.

STEP 1: What is the verb? It is *was reviewed.*

STEP 2: Who is performing the action of portraying? *Him* is. Notice that the pronoun *him* is in the objective case (meaning it fills the role of *object* in a sentence). To revise the sentence with the pronoun as *subject,* we need a pronoun in the nominative case. Therefore, we will use *he,* not *him,* in the active voice sentence.

STEP 3: In active voice, the sentence is *He reviewed the film.* (NOT *Him reviewed the film*)

EXAMPLE 4

Shakespeare is misled about Thomas Kent's identity.

STEP 1: What is the verb? It is *is misled.*

STEP 2: Who is performing the action of misleading Shakespeare? The sentence does not specify. To supply a subject for the active voice version, draw upon your knowledge of the subject. In the *Shakespeare* movie, Viola pretends to be a male actor, Thomas Kent.

STEP 3: In active voice, the sentence is *Viola misleads Shakespeare about Thomas Kent's identity.*

ACTIVITY 7

Look back at the sentences you labeled *passive* in Activity 6. On the lines below, rewrite each of these sentences in the active voice. If the passive sentence does not specify who performs the action, choose your own subject for the revision.

Sample:

*Note: The sample below is a revision of sample **a** in Activity 6.*

Actress Julia Stiles has earned my admiration.

1. _____

2. _____

3. _____

4. _____

5. _____

6. _____

 Writing Application

Active and Passive Voice

Think about a movie or television show you saw recently, or book you recently read. Specifically, think about events that happened in the plot. On a separate sheet of paper, write five sentences in the **passive voice** about the movie or book plot. You can refer to the examples regarding *Shakespeare in Love* for ideas.

With your teacher's approval, exchange papers with a classmate. Revise each of your classmate's passive voice sentences to be in the active voice. Share the results.

QUESTION: Is it ever okay to use passive voice?

ANSWER: Yes. Passive voice has certain useful purposes. When you want to emphasize the person or thing acted upon, use the passive voice.

EXAMPLE: *Shakespeare in Love* has been released on DVD.

(Readers don't care who released the movie. Rather, they want to know something about the movie itself. Therefore, the writer of this sentence places emphasis on *Shakespeare in Love* by putting this noun in the subject position.)

Passive voice sentences are also appropriate when the performer of the action is unknown, or the writer does not want to reveal who performed the action.

EXAMPLES: Thirteen DVDs were stolen.

(The writer does not know who stole the DVDs.)

The day manager has been accused of the theft.

(The writer does not want to reveal who accused the manager.)

ACTIVITY 8

Decide whether each sentence should be rewritten in the active voice. Write necessary revisions on the lines provided. If the sentence should remain unchanged, write *no change* on the line.

> **Samples:**
>
> **a.** Sometimes, a kid's dreams are not understood by parents.
>
> _Sometimes, parents do not understand a kid's dreams._
>
> **b.** Dreams should be nurtured despite opposition.
>
> _no change_

1. In *Billy Elliot,* boxing lessons are abandoned by Billy.

_____

2. Ballet lessons are taken by him instead.

_____

3. His dad, a manly miner, is shocked by the choice.

_____

4. The story is set in northern England.

_____

5. The wisdom of Billy's choice is revealed by this unforgettable movie.

_____

3 Sentence Variety

To keep a reader's interest, sentences must not always follow a set pattern. Good sentences are varied in length and structure.

MONOTONOUS:	Carl Lewis is a sports legend. He won nine Olympic gold medals. He is my hero.
VARIED:	Carl Lewis, my hero, is a sports legend who won nine Olympic gold medals.
VARIED:	The sports legend Carl Lewis, who won nine Olympic gold medals, is my hero.
MONOTONOUS:	Lewis went to the Olympics in 1984. The Games were in Los Angeles. He won four gold medals.
VARIED:	In 1984, Lewis won not one but four Olympic gold medals at the Games in Los Angeles.
VARIED:	At the 1984 Games in Los Angeles, Lewis won not one but four Olympic gold medals.

Sentence Length and Purpose

As you learned in Lesson 2, conciseness is always a desirable goal. By avoiding padding and unnecessary words, you can create a concise sentence. However, concise sentences are not necessarily short ones. The following sentences use words economically, but they vary in length.

SHORT:	Carl Lewis was born into an athletic family.
LONGER:	At Tuskegee Institute, his parents had excelled at track and other sports.
STILL LONGER:	Lewis first qualified as an Olympic athlete in 1980; however, that year the United States boycotted the Games, held in Moscow.

✏️ **Writing Application** Varying Sentence Length

On a separate sheet of paper, write **six to eight** sentences about a sport or other activity (such as band, debate, woodworking, etc.) that interests you, whether it is a competitive activity like football or a pastime like walking in the park. Vary your sentences' lengths to include short sentences, longer sentences, and still longer ones. Make sure that each sentence, no matter its length, is concise.

You can also vary the purpose of sentences. Most sentences are declarative; their purpose is to inform. For variety, use an occasional question, exclamation, or command, but don't overdo.

QUESTION: When did Lewis retire from competition?

EXCLAMATION: What an amazing athlete he is!

COMMAND: Look at this Web site on Carl Lewis.

POLITE REQUEST: Please write down the URL for me.

ACTIVITY 1 _____

Revise each of the following sentences according to the directions given in parentheses. Write the revision on the lines provided.

Samples:

a. I am curious about what Carl Lewis is doing nowadays. *(Make a question.)*

What is Carl Lewis doing nowadays?

b. You chose an interesting research topic. *(Make an exclamation.)*

What an interesting research topic you chose!

1. People may wonder how Carl Lewis got started in sports. *(Ask a question.)*

_____

_____

2. During the research process, students should document each source they consult. *(Make a command.)*

_____

_____

3. Each student should give his or her essay an interesting title. *(Make a polite request.)*

_____

_____

4. Lewis has been an inspiration to other athletes. *(Make an exclamation.)*

_____

_____

5. There is a question about what aspect of his training was hardest for Lewis. *(Ask a question.)*

_____

_____

Sentence Structure

You can avoid monotony by varying sentence beginnings, by using appositives, and by using verbals (participles, infinitives, and gerunds).

Every sentence does not have to begin with the subject. When a shift in placement is both natural and effective, begin a sentence with a word other than the subject. Formations that can work well at the start of a sentence are listed below.

ADVERB:	*Undoubtedly,* Babe Didrikson Zaharias was one of the greatest female athletes of the twentieth century.
ADVERB PHRASE:	*From 1930 to 1932,* she played basketball for the women's All-America team.
ADVERB CLAUSE:	*When she wasn't playing ball*, she competed in track-and-field events.
THERE:	*There* was no end to Babe's interest in sports. (Note: Do not overdo. Beginning with *There* is often not the strongest option.)
PREPOSITIONAL PHRASE:	*At the 1932 Olympic Games,* she won gold in the 80-meter hurdles and in the javelin throw.
PARTICIPIAL PHRASE:	*Competing as a team by herself,* she won the team title in the 1932 Women's Amateur Athletic Association.
INFINITIVE PHRASE:	*To expand her athletic skills,* Babe played baseball, softball, and football; swam; and figure-skated.
PREPOSITIONAL PHRASE WITH GERUND:	*After marrying George Zaharias,* Babe took up golf in 1938.
APPOSITIVE:	*An amateur golfer,* Babe won eighteen golf championships.
VERB:	*Cheering* her on *were* countless fans.

KEY TERMS

adverb: A word that modifies a verb, an adjective, or an adverb.

appositive: A word or word group that identifies or renames a noun or pronoun.

gerund: A verb form used as a noun. A gerund ends in *ing*.

infinitive: A verb form that can be used as a noun, an adjective, or an adverb. Most infinitives begin with *to*, as in *to eat*.

participle: A verb form that may be used as part of a verb phrase or as an adjective.

phrase: A related sequence of words that does not have both a subject and its verb.

ACTIVITY 2

Revise each sentence by moving a word or word group before the subject.

Samples:

a. Some children learn a sport before they can read.

   Before they can read, some children learn a sport.

b. Tiger's parents taught him golf at age two to give their son a head start.

   To give their son a head start, Tiger's parents taught him golf at age two.

1. Eldrick Woods, nicknamed Tiger, is one of the most impressive U.S. golfers.

_____

_____

2. Tiger won the 1991 U.S. Junior Amateur championship at age fifteen.

_____

_____

3. He won the next two championships too, returning in 1992 and 1993.

_____

_____

4. Tiger consistently hits golf balls more than three hundred yards.

_____

_____

5. Tiger won the 1996 collegiate title after he enrolled in Stanford University.

_____

_____

6. He turned pro after leaving college in August 1996.

_____

_____

7. A great deal of prize money is there in the major golf tournaments.

_____

_____

8. Tiger won over six million dollars in one season.

_____

_____

9. His parents are proudly watching Tiger's career.

_____

_____

10. Tiger won the Masters, the U.S. Open, the British Open, and the PGA Championships to complete the "Grand Slam" in 2001.

_____

_____

Composition Hint

You can use sentence structure to place emphasis on one part of the sentence over another. Compare these examples from Activity 2:

Some children learn a sport before they can read.

(This sentence emphasizes learning a sport.)

Before they can read, some children learn a sport.

(This sentence emphasizes the time factor of when children learn a sport by placing the *Before* clause first.)

Writing Application — Using Sentence Structure to Vary Emphasis

Look back at the sentences in Activity 2. In each pair of sentences, both the original and your rewritten version express the same basic thought. However, each has a different emphasis based on the sentence's structure.

On a separate sheet of paper, explain whether you prefer the original or the rewritten version of the ten sentences in Activity 2, and why. Here is an example based on sample sentence b:

b. The original version states that the parents taught Tiger golf at age two, but the real question I had was <u>why</u> they did this. Therefore, I like the rewritten version, which emphasizes why they did this by placing the infinitive phrase first.

Another way to vary sentence structure is to use an appositive within the sentence.

WITHOUT APPOSITIVE: Gertrude Ederle set her sights on the English Channel in 1925.

WITH APPOSITIVE: Gertrude Ederle, *an avid swimmer,* set her sights on the English Channel in 1925.

WITHOUT APPOSITIVE: The English Channel is about thirty-five miles across.

WITH APPOSITIVE: The English Channel, *a strait between England and France,* is about thirty-five miles across.

Look again at the two sentences with appositives above. Notice that each appositive is set off by a comma before it and a comma after it. If an appositive falls at the end of a sentence, use a period instead of the second comma.

EXAMPLE: One of my heroes is Gertrude Ederle, *an amazing swimmer.*

ACTIVITY 3

Rewrite each sentence, adding an appositive. Choose from the appositives listed below, and use each one only once. Remember that an appositive is set off by commas, as shown in the sample sentence.

a born champion	fourteen hours and thirty-one minutes
~~an American~~	the year of her first attempt
Gertrude's hometown	a cape in France

1. In 1925 Gertrude was unsuccessful.

_____

_____

2. But this young swimmer did not give up.

_____

_____

3. In 1926 she set out from Gris-Nez and swam successfully across the channel.

_____

_____

4. Her swim time beat the men's world record by nearly two hours.

_____

_____

5. New York City gave her a ticker-tape parade.

_____

_____

Another way to vary sentence structure is to use verbals and verbal phrases.

WITHOUT PARTICIPLE:	Sammy Sosa was born in the Dominican Republic. Sammy became a baseball star in the United States.
WITH PARTICIPIAL PHRASE:	_Born in the Dominican Republic,_ Sammy Sosa became a baseball star in the United States.
WITHOUT GERUND:	Sammy was signed by the Texas Rangers after he had turned sixteen.
WITH GERUND PHRASE:	Sammy was signed by the Texas Rangers _after turning_ sixteen.
WITHOUT INFINITIVE:	He played for minor-league teams. He acquired the skills necessary for major-league ball.
WITH INFINITIVE PHRASE:	He played for minor-league teams _to acquire_ the skills necessary for major-league ball.

ACTIVITY 4 _____

Combine each set of monotonous sentences to create one sentence with engaging structure. A hint in parentheses tells you what is needed. Write on the lines provided.

> **Samples:**
>
> **a.** Sammy landed 30 homers and 30 stolen bases in one season.
>
> He earned a place in the "30-30 club." *(participial phrase)*
>
> <u>Sammy landed 30 homers and 30 stolen bases in one season, earning a place</u>
>
> <u>in the "30-30 club."</u>
>
> **b.** He earned this level of success. *(gerund phrase)*
>
> It was incredibly difficult.
>
> <u>Earning this level of success was incredibly difficult.</u>

1. Sammy earned the Rangers' esteem. *(participial phrase)*

He played his first major-league game in June 1989.

_____

_____

2. He attacked the ball forcefully. *(gerund phrase)*

This was his batting style.

_____

_____

3. The Rangers sent Sammy back to the minor leagues in order that he improve his batting. *(Make the words after **leagues** an infinitive phrase.)*

_____

_____

4. Then the Rangers made a decision.

They traded Sammy to the Chicago White Sox. *(infinitive phrase)*

_____

_____

5. He won Chicago's starting right field position. *(participial phrase)*

He played strong all year.

_____

_____

6. He performed poorly the next season.

He let his old batting habits return. *(participial phrase)*

_____

_____

7. Chicago sent Sammy back to the minor leagues. *(gerund phrase)*

This was Chicago's solution.

_____

_____

8. Later in the season Sammy received an offer.

The offer was for a return to the White Sox. *(infinitive phrase)*

_____

_____

9. Finally, Sammy was learning.

He must watch the ball better. *(infinitive phrase)*

He must bat with skill, not with aggression. *(infinitive phrase)*

_____

_____

10. Slowly he earned respect and fame.

He became a true baseball star. *(participial phrase—either sentence)*

_____

_____

Review of Sentence Composition

Recall the four types of sentences:
- A *simple sentence* contains one main clause and no subordinate clauses.
- A *compound sentence* contains two or more main clauses and no subordinate clauses.
- A *complex sentence* has one main clause and at least one subordinate clause.
- A *compound-complex sentence* has at least two main clauses and at least one subordinate clause.

ACTIVITY 1 _____

Combine each set of sentences to form one strong simple or compound sentence. Write on the lines provided.

> **Samples:**
>
> **a.** Buddy Holly recorded innovative rock and roll.
>
> He rose to fame in the late 1950s.
>
> <u>Buddy Holly recorded innovative rock and roll and rose to fame in the</u>
>
> <u>late 1950s.</u>
>
> **b.** Buddy Holly's career was soaring.
>
> His life was cut short by a plane crash.
>
> <u>Buddy Holly's career was soaring, but his life was cut short by a plane crash.</u>

1. Buddy Holly was one of America's early rock stars.

   Elvis Presley was also one of this country's early rock stars.

   _____

   _____

2. As a youngster, Buddy developed a passion for music.

   Rock and roll and rhythm and blues inspired his musical creativity.

   _____

   _____

3. Buddy listened to records by Elvis, Bo Diddley, and others.

   He began developing his own personal style.

   _____

   _____

4. In 1957, Buddy joined with three other musicians.

The foursome formed The Crickets.

_____

_____

5. The group recorded several hits.

The biggest was probably "Peggy Sue."

_____

_____

Writing Application

Simple and Compound Sentences

On a separate sheet of paper, write **five or six** sentences about a musical artist whom you admire. Tell who the artist is, what kind of music he or she plays, and why you admire this person. Make your sentences powerful by varying their structure in the following ways: In two of the simple sentences, use compound elements (compound subject and/or compound verb); in addition, use at least two compound sentences. Above each sentence, label it *simple* or *compound*.

ACTIVITY 2

Combine each set of sentences to form one strong complex or compound-complex sentence. Write on the lines provided.

Samples:

a. America is home to a world of music styles.

These music styles include rock, African, Latin, and others.

America is home to a world of music styles, which include rock, African, Latin, and others.

b. Many Latin singers first sang in Spanish.

They have reached the top of the charts.

Later they crossed over to English.

Many Latin singers who have reached the top of the charts first sang in Spanish, and later they crossed over to English.

1. Latin pop music exploded onto the music scene in 1999.

   Ricky Martin, Jennifer Lopez, and others released big hits.

   _____

   _____

2. Ricky Martin sang "Livin' la Vida Loca."

   Jennifer Lopez sang "If You Had My Love."

   Lopez was also an actress.

   _____

   _____

3. Both of these songs reached number one on the charts.

   These songs appeared repeatedly on MTV.

   _____

   _____

4. Other Latino artists were Gloria Estefan, Julio Iglesias, and Shakira.

   These artists gained national recognition.

   _____

   _____

5. America's love of Latin music did not end.

   The first wave of Latin hits dropped off the charts.

   Instead, it increased thanks to Marc Anthony and many others.

   _____

   _____

Writing Application

Simple and Compound Sentences

What is your favorite kind of music, and why? On a separate sheet of paper, write **five** sentences explaining your answers to these questions. Use at least two complex sentences and at least one compound-complex sentence, and label each one.

Recall the characteristics of strong, forceful sentences:

_____ conciseness

_____ clarity and specificity

_____ unity

_____ active voice unless there is a specific reason for passive voice

_____ sentence variety in length and structure

ACTIVITY 3 _____

Revise each sentence to correct errors in conciseness, clarity and specificity, or unity. Write on the lines provided.

Samples:

a. Music fans always welcome songs that are fresh, memorable, and ones that are not like others because they are one of a kind.

   Music fans always welcome songs that are fresh, memorable, and unique.

b. Based on the fact that I am cognizant that CDs can be expensive, I buy them used.

   Because CDs can be expensive, I buy them used.

1. Each and every time I turn on the radio to listen to it, I hear the new Ashlee Simpson song.

   _____

   _____

2. Despite the fact that she is popular, I wonder if her celebrity status will last.

   _____

   _____

3. I endeavor to be equitable in my evaluation of music; I procure only the best CDs.

   _____

   _____

4. Sometimes a hit song is sung by an artist who is new and who we think is the next big thing but whom we forget within a year, which is too bad.

   _____

   _____

5. Ashlee's fame is helped by her sister, who is Jessica Simpson, who is also a singer, who starred in her own TV show, which was called *Newlyweds.*

_____

_____

6. Her music is good too.

_____

_____

7. I wonder if Jessica won't be remembered five years from now.

_____

_____

8. This Simpson sister is already known for her beauty, her singing, and she is humorous.

_____

_____

9. Because Ashlee did publicity for her album, she dyed her blonde hair dark brown.

_____

_____

10. Ashlee is a brunette, or Jessica is a blonde.

_____

_____

ACTIVITY 4 _____

Decide whether each sentence would be stronger in the active voice. If yes, rewrite the sentence in active voice. If no, write *no change.* Write on the lines provided.

> **Samples:**
>
> **a.** Many types of piano music were composed by Frédéric Chopin.
>
> *Frédéric Chopin composed many types of piano music.* _____
>
> **b.** His compositions are celebrated for their beauty, sensitivity, and originality.
>
> *no change* _____

1. Chopin is known for his nocturnes, etudes, and mazurkas.

_____

_____

2. Six-year-old Frédéric was given piano lessons by Adalbert Zywny.

_____

_____

3. Master composers were studied by them, including Bach and Mozart.

_____

_____

4. New methods of playing music on the piano were invented by Chopin.

_____

_____

5. Two centuries later, Chopin's music is still respected, studied, and enjoyed.

_____

_____

ACTIVITY 5 _____

Revise each sentence or set of sentences to create variety in structure. To do so, vary the sentence beginning or use an appositive, participle, gerund, or infinitive. Write on the lines provided.

> **Samples:**
>
> **a.** Vanessa Williams won a beauty pageant in 1983. This was just the beginning. She was talented.
>
> _Winning a beauty pageant in 1983 was just the beginning for the talented_
>
> _Vanessa Williams._
>
> **b.** At the time she was young. She was inexperienced. She soon learned. She took charge of her destiny.
>
> _Young and inexperienced, she soon learned to take charge of her destiny._

1. The first black Miss America was more than just a beauty queen. The first black Miss America was Vanessa Williams.

_____

_____

2. Her first music album was released in 1988. _The Right Stuff_ went gold.

_____

_____

3. She continued to record and perform. She also married and started a family.

_____

_____

4. She began other artistic endeavors. She acted. She danced.

_____

_____

5. She acted. She danced. She sang. These things brought her respect and stardom.

_____

_____

Sentence Composition

The following research applications encourage you to take **sentence** composition beyond this workbook and into real life. Each assignment asks you to gather information on one of the themes in the previous lessons and to write clear, forceful sentences about your findings. Enjoy your research and take pride in using your skills of sentence composition!

THEME: American Folklore

SKILL: Using the Four Sentence Types

Choose an American folklore character who actually existed, such as one of those named in Lesson 1 or another that interests you. In the library and/or on the Internet, find out details regarding this person's place in folklore. What actions or character traits made the person a folk hero? What kind of literature (poems, ballads, stories, etc.) has been written about him or her? If the character has a nickname (such as "Calamity Jane"), find out what inspired it.

Next, use your research to write **one long** paragraph (around ten sentences) or **two shorter** paragraphs (around five sentences each) about your chosen character. In the paragraphs, answer the questions asked above and provide any other details that help paint a picture of the person. In your writing, use each of the four sentence types at least once. Label your sentences S for *simple,* CD for *compound,* CX for *complex,* or Cd-Cx for *compound-complex.*

THEME: Film

SKILL: Writing Clear, Forceful Sentences

Go online to research viewers' responses to a movie that is rated PG-13 or lower. To get started, you might look up the movie on the Internet Movie Database (www.imdb.com) or on a merchant site such as www.amazon.com. These sites post people's personal reviews, opinions, and comments.

After reviewing the movie's plot and reading reviewers' comments, write **two** paragraphs of around five to seven sentences each. Briefly summarize the movie's plot or theme, and then describe how people have responded to the movie. Make sure each sentence you write is concise, clear, unified, and, if necessary, in the active voice.

THEME: Sports

SKILL: Creating Sentence Variety

Choose a sports hero, such as one of those named in Lesson 3 or another who interests you. In the library and/or on the Internet, find out details regarding this person's claim to fame. Which sport or sports does he or she play? In which major events has the person competed and what were the outcomes? What particular challenge has this person faced in the rise to fame?

Next, use your research to write **two** paragraphs of around five to seven sentences each about this sports hero. In the paragraphs, answer some or all of the questions above and provide any other details that help paint a picture of this hero. In your writing, vary sentence length and structure to create a pleasing variety.

THEME: Music

SKILL: Writing Strong, Varied Sentences

Biographical profiles of celebrities are popular in magazines, on television, and on Web sites. To write your own celebrity profile, first choose a musical artist who interests you, either one of those named in Lesson 4 or someone else. Then research the basic facts of this person's life. Where and when was the artist born? Educated? What song or album is he or she known for? What particular challenge has the artist faced? What is next in this person's career?

Good sources of biographical information are encyclopedia articles (online or in print), short biographies (in the nonfiction section of a library), and official fan sites on the Internet. Gather solid, reliable information, and write **two or three** paragraphs of five to seven sentences each. Polish the profile by making sure each sentence is clear and forceful and by varying the length and structure of sentences.

Sentence Composition

PART 1 _____

Directions: Circle the letter of the best revision of each sentence or set of sentences and write it on the blank. If the item is already clear and forceful, choose the letter for *NO CHANGE*.

1. In the event that you are asked to present a speech, remember these tips that are helpful.

   A. NO CHANGE

   B. If you are asked to present a speech, bear in mind these tips that are really quite helpful.

   C. If you are asked to present a speech, remember these helpful tips.

   D. You may be asked to present a speech. Remember these tips. They are helpful.

2. You must practice your speech. This must be done out loud. The optimum time to carry out this practice is ahead of time.

   F. NO CHANGE

   G. Practice your speech aloud ahead of time.

   H. You must practice your speech. This must be done out loud ahead of time.

   J. Practicing your speech must be done out loud. Carrying out this practice ahead of time is optimum.

3. During the speech, use suitable hand gestures and make eye contact with the audience.

   A. NO CHANGE

   B. During the speech, use suitable hand gestures. Make eye contact with the audience.

   C. These things must be done during the speech. For one thing, use suitable hand gestures. Another helpful thing is to make eye contact with the audience.

   D. Use hand gestures. Make eye contact.

4. Some activities that are mistakes are jingling pocket change, which is distracting, and messing with your hair, which make you look nervous, and fiddling with your jacket or tie, which distracts from what you are saying.

   F. NO CHANGE

   G. Some activities that are mistakes are jingling pocket change, which is distracting. Another is messing with your hair. It makes you look nervous. Fiddling with your jacket or tie distracts from what you are saying.

   H. Distracting activities include jingling pocket change, messing with your hair, and fiddling with your clothing.

   J. Jingling pocket change is distracting, and messing with your hair makes you look nervous, and fiddling with your jacket or tie distracts from what you are saying.

5. The pitch and volume of your voice should be varied. This will help hold listeners' attention.

    A. NO CHANGE

    B. To vary the pitch and volume of your voice, hold listeners' attention.

    C. Vary the pitch and volume of your voice to hold listeners' attention.

    D. The pitch and volume of your voice should be varied to hold listeners' attention.

PART 2

Directions: In each item, circle the letter of the sentence that is more clear and forceful. On the lines provided, write one or two sentences explaining why it is the stronger of the two. For example, you might explain that one choice is more concise, uses parallel structure, uses an accurate connective, etc.

6.   **a.** If possible, the room should be checked out by the speaker ahead of time.

    b. If possible, the speaker should check out the room ahead of time.

_____

_____

7.   **a.** Standing behind the podium may facilitate one's level of comfort.

    b. Standing behind the podium may be comfortable.

_____

_____

8.   **a.** Good speakers prepare visual aids, but they don't overdo.

    b. Good speakers prepare visual aids, and they don't overdo.

_____

_____

9.   **a.** Stage fright, a common challenge, can be managed.

    b. Stage fright is a common challenge. It can be managed.

_____

_____

10. **a.** You can manage stage fright. You can pause occasionally and take a few deep breaths.

    b. To manage stage fright, pause occasionally and take a few deep breaths.

_____

_____

2 Sentence Revision

In Part One, we examined qualities of strong sentences. Focusing on the types of sentences and their structures, those lessons outlined how to manipulate sentence elements for maximum strength. Now we turn to another aspect of building strong sentences: getting the grammar and mechanics right.

Specifically, the following lessons show you how to ensure a sentence is complete; how to check for common grammar errors; and how to check for errors in punctuation, capitalization, and spelling (otherwise known as "mechanics"). The lessons culminate in a master checklist for sentence revision, which you can use any time you write sentences.

5 Sentence Errors

Three common errors in sentences are the *sentence fragment,* the *run-on,* and the *comma splice* (a type of run-on). All of these errors are serious; however, all have clear solutions for revision.

Sentence Fragments

Each of the following examples begins with a capital letter and has end punctuation, yet none is a complete sentence. They are fragments.

FRAGMENTS: A new telephone with numerous special features. (no verb)

Of course, rings with a special musical tone. (no subject)

There on the desk, beside the computer. (no subject or verb)

 A *sentence fragment* is a word group punctuated as a sentence yet lacking a subject, a verb, or both.

Study these additional examples of fragments, along with examples of how each can be revised to be a complete sentence.

NO VERB: Computers in every office nowadays.

COMPLETE SENTENCE: Computers *are present* in every office nowadays.

NO VERB: Without a doubt, technology making our lives easier.

(The word *making* by itself is not a verb. It needs a helping verb such as *is.*)

COMPLETE SENTENCE: Without a doubt, technology *is* making our lives easier.

NO SUBJECT: Confused me with all those buttons.

COMPLETE SENTENCE: *The fax machine* confused me with all those buttons.

NO SUBJECT, NO VERB: In the tray underneath the printer.

(This fragment consists of two prepositional phrases.)

COMPLETE SENTENCE: *Please insert paper* in the tray underneath the printer.

(In this revision, the understood subject is *you.*)

Revise each fragment to be a complete sentence. Add whatever words are necessary, writing on the lines provided.

> **Samples:**
>
> **a.** Sometimes, cell phones worth their weight in gold.
>
> Sometimes, cell phones can be worth their weight in gold.
>
> **b.** In a difficult situation and in need of assistance.
>
> A cell phone can be used to get help for a person in a difficult situation
>
> and in need of assistance.

1. Driving down the road to school.

2. All of a sudden, a flat tire.

3. Must change it and get to school on time.

4. Unfortunately, rain coming down in torrents.

5. Beside the road on a flat, grassy area.

6. The spare tire in the trunk, under a lot of junk.

7. Filled with despair at ever getting this fixed on time.

8. A solution to this entire problem.

_____

_____

9. To call the auto club on this handy cell phone.

_____

_____

10. Ten minutes later, a professional on the scene.

_____

_____

QUESTION: A subordinate clause has a subject and a verb. Can it stand alone as a sentence?

ANSWER: No, it cannot stand alone. A subordinate clause by itself is a sentence fragment.

SUBORDINATE CLAUSE: When I want to go to a movie.

COMPLETE SENTENCE: When I want to go to a movie, I check the movie listings.

SUBORDINATE CLAUSE: What time a certain film starts.

COMPLETE SENTENCE: The listings tell me what time a certain film starts.

SUBORDINATE CLAUSE: Whenever a new comedy comes out.

COMPLETE SENTENCE: Whenever a new comedy comes out, I am first in line.

SUBORDINATE CLAUSE: Because a movie should entertain, not sadden you.

COMPLETE SENTENCE: I prefer comedies because a movie should entertain, not sadden you.

In your writing, be especially watchful for subordinate clauses that stand alone as sentences (such as those in the examples above). This kind of fragment is common yet easily fixed.

QUESTION: How can I revise a subordinate clause to be a complete sentence?

ANSWER: You can (1) add a main clause or (2) remove the subordinating conjunction or relative pronoun that introduces the subordinate clause. Here are a few examples:

SUBORDINATE CLAUSE: Where a movie is showing.

COMPLETE SENTENCE: The listings tell me where a movie is showing.

(Add a main clause to create a complete sentence.)

SUBORDINATE CLAUSE: Although a film may be showing in several locations.

COMPLETE SENTENCE: A film may be showing in several locations.

(Remove _Although_ to create a complete sentence.)

SUBORDINATE CLAUSE: Web sites that provide show times and locations.

(This word group has a subject, *Web sites,* and a subordinate clause. Because there is no verb, the word group is a fragment.)

COMPLETE SENTENCE: Web sites provide show times and locations.

(Remove *that* to create a complete sentence.)

ACTIVITY 2

Revise each fragment to make it a complete sentence. Add or remove words as necessary. Write the revised sentence on the lines provided.

Samples:

a. Which is also called a URL.

The address of a Web site is also called a URL.

b. Schools that have attractive Web sites.

Schools that have attractive Web sites may attract new students.

1. If you need to find out information.

_____

_____

2. When the page of search results comes up.

_____

_____

3. So that you can locate facts quickly and easily.

_____

_____

4. Which is one common use for the Internet.

_____

_____

5. Unless you'd rather buy a newspaper.

_____

_____

6. Because searching the Internet is convenient.

_____

_____

7. Whoever doesn't own a computer.

_____

_____

8. When a school or public library is open.

_____

_____

9. Colleges that interest you.

_____

_____

10. Whether you want to send in an application.

_____

_____

Run-on Sentences

When two sentences are run together with no punctuation or conjunction separating them, the result is a _run-on._ (Run-ons are also known as "fused sentences.")

 A _run-on sentence_ **consists of two or more sentences run together without punctuation or a conjunction between them.**

RUN-ON: Cell phones are not just for emergencies they are essential to everyday communication.

CORRECT: Cell phones are not just for emergencies. They are essential to everyday communication.

RUN-ON: The sales clerk didn't just show me the expensive models she showed me the basic ones too.

CORRECT: The sales clerk didn't just show me the expensive models. She showed me the basic ones too.

QUESTION: How can I revise a run-on to be correct?

ANSWER: You have several options for revision, as explained below.

(1) Separate the sentences with an end mark or, if they are closely related in meaning, with a semicolon. Examples of using a period are shown above, in the sentences about cell phones. Below is an example of using a semicolon.

RUN-ON: Sometimes I need to stay late at school calling Mom on my cell is easy.

CORRECT: Sometimes I need to stay late at school; calling Mom on my cell is easy.

(2) Separate the sentences with a comma and a conjunction.

RUN-ON: I could not live without my cell phone it comes in handy daily.

CORRECT: I could not live without my cell phone, for it comes in handy daily.

RUN-ON: Dad bought me the phone I pay for the service myself.

CORRECT: Dad bought me the phone, but I pay for the service myself.

(3) Revise one sentence to be a subordinate clause properly joined to the other sentence. The result is a complex sentence.

RUN-ON: I could not live without my cell phone it comes in handy daily.

CORRECT: I could not live without my cell phone because it comes in handy daily.

RUN-ON: I go on dates without fail I take my cell phone.

CORRECT: Whenever I go on dates, without fail I take my cell phone.

ACTIVITY 3

On the lines provided, revise each run-on sentence to make it one or more correct sentences.

> **Samples:**
>
> **a.** This phone is surprisingly small it fits right in my back pocket.
>
> This phone is surprisingly small. It fits right in my back pocket.
>
> **b.** Using pay phones was an annoyance they weren't always convenient.
>
> Using pay phones was an annoyance because they weren't always convenient.

1. You are at the store you forgot the shopping list.

_____

_____

2. The solution is simple just call home on your cell.

_____

_____

3. I went to the mall on a Friday night no one I know was there.

_____

_____

4. In my pocket was my tiny phone immediately it linked me with a friend.

_____

_____

5. Standing in line at the driver's license office is boring I'd rather be talking to a friend.

_____

_____

6. The boredom is lessened I pull out my trusty phone.

_____

_____

7. One day I was shopping in a home improvement warehouse with Mom we lost each other.

_____

_____

8. She called me on my cell quickly we found each other.

_____

_____

9. Driving at night is never a problem my cell is beside me at all times.

_____

_____

10. Most of all, I enjoy calling my sweetie the number is in my speed dial.

_____

_____

Comma Splices

A specific kind of run-on sentence is the _comma splice._

 A **_comma splice_ results when two or more sentences are joined with only a comma.**

A comma by itself cannot properly join, or splice together, two sentences.

COMMA SPLICE: Save up your money, buy your own DVD player.

CORRECT: Save up your money. Buy your own DVD player.

               (A period separates the sentences.)

CORRECT: Save up your money, _and_ buy your own DVD player.

               (The conjunction _and_ works with the comma to join the sentences.)

COMMA SPLICE:	Basketball sneakers can cost seventy-five dollars, a DVD player costs less.
CORRECT:	Basketball sneakers can cost seventy-five dollars, *but* a DVD player costs less.
	(The conjunction *but* works with the comma to join the sentences.)
COMMA SPLICE:	One model costs fifty dollars, the other costs forty-five.
CORRECT:	One model costs fifty dollars; the other costs forty-five.
	(A semicolon joins the sentences.)

QUESTION: How can I revise a comma splice to be a complete, correct sentence?

ANSWER: Your options are similar to those used to correct run-ons.

(1) Separate the sentences with an end mark or a semicolon.

COMMA SPLICE:	Francine got a weekend job, she cleans houses.
CORRECT:	Francine got a weekend job. She cleans houses.
COMMA SPLICE:	She is saving her paychecks carefully, soon she will be able to afford a few nice things.
CORRECT:	She is saving her paychecks carefully; soon she will be able to afford a few nice things.

(2) Add a conjunction.

COMMA SPLICE:	Modern technology can seem expensive, one or two items can be affordable.
CORRECT:	Modern technology can seem expensive, *but* one or two items can be affordable.
COMMA SPLICE:	Decide on one nice thing to buy, save your money faithfully.
CORRECT:	Decide on one nice thing to buy, *and* save your money faithfully.

(3) Revise one sentence to be a subordinate clause properly joined to the other sentence.

COMMA SPLICE:	You are in school, holding a job may seem difficult.
CORRECT:	*When* you are in school, holding a job may seem difficult.
COMMA SPLICE:	A job doesn't have to overwhelm you, work part time.
CORRECT:	A job doesn't have to overwhelm you *if* you work part time.

Note: For help deciding which subordinating conjunction to use in a revision, you can review the Composition Hint and the table of conjunctions that follows it on pages 11–12.

In making any of the revisions described above, be sure you use correct punctuation (commas, semicolons, etc.). On pages 78 and 79, you will find a table listing guidelines for using punctuation.

On the lines provided, revise each comma splice to be one or more correct sentences.

> **Samples:**
>
> **a.** Some people complain about the cost of new things, they should think creatively.
>
> <u>Some people complain about the cost of new things, but they should</u>
>
> <u>think creatively.</u>
>
> **b.** Anyone can save up money, allowance and paychecks are two sources of funds.
>
> <u>Anyone can save up money. Allowance and paychecks are two sources</u>
>
> <u>of funds.</u>

1. What is more important to you, would you rather have fancy shoes or a television?

_____

_____

2. Wear last year's sneakers, spend your money on something more useful.

_____

_____

3. You are a college student, pool some money with your roommate.

_____

_____

4. You are living at home, ask a sibling to share the cost of an expensive item.

_____

_____

5. How much do you spend on fancy coffee drinks, could you save half of that?

_____

_____

6. Magazines and makeup cost a lot, limiting these purchases saves money.

_____

_____

7. You can read magazines in a library, it doesn't cost a thing.

_____

_____

8. It may take a while to save sufficient money, you can do it.

_____

_____

9. A CD player and a television are fun to own, they provide entertainment.

_____

_____

10. Host a movie night, ask a friend to bring his DVD player.

_____

_____

ACTIVITY 5

Find and correct the comma splices in the following passage. Make revisions by crossing out errors and writing corrections above them. The first comma splice is corrected for you as a sample. You should find four additional comma splices.

In my opinion, some forms of modern technology are easier to use than others; ~~for~~

example, take the Internet itself. It's easy to open a Web browser and type in a search term

or a URL. Most cell phones are also user-friendly, some certainly have a lot of buttons.

DVD players and digital cameras are no problem, they are so easy to figure out.

Other high-tech inventions can be downright confusing, a good example is download-

able music. I know that something called an iPod or MP3 player stores the tunes, but how

do you get the tunes into the player? Is it like burning a CD? Once the tunes are in the

player, how do you organize them and search for the one you want to play? These are

questions I cannot answer, for this reason, I need a tutorial from a friend.

Writing Application

Writing Complete, Correct Sentences

What form of modern technology can you not live without? Maybe you can't live without your cell phone, or maybe you are addicted to surfing the Internet. Perhaps you never leave home without your MP3 player. Whatever your favorite gadget or service, think about why you value it so much. Then write a paragraph of **nine or ten** sentences explaining what form of technology you value most and why. Check each sentence to ensure it is complete and correct, making revisions as necessary.

Grammar Errors in Sentences

Using correct grammar is about more than getting good grades. It is also about gaining the trust of readers, expressing ideas in an appealing manner, and avoiding ambiguity and confusion. Even the best of writers must edit their sentences for grammar errors. This lesson explains some of the most common errors in the usage of verbs, modifiers, and pronouns.

Verbs

To verify that you have used verbs correctly in your sentences, ask yourself a few simple questions.

1. Is the verb in its correct form?

A regular verb forms its past tense by adding *d* or *ed* to the base form. For example, the past tense of *walk* is *walked.* The past tense of *smile* is *smiled.* However, irregular verbs form their past tense forms in other ways. For example, you wouldn't write *I **speaked** to Angie yesterday.* You would write *I **spoke** to Angie yesterday.*

Study the following table of sixteen common irregular verbs and their past and past participle forms. (The past participle is always used with a form of *has;* for this reason, the word *has* is printed in the chart with each past participle form.)

16 IRREGULAR VERBS

BASE FORM	PAST	PAST PARTICIPLE
bring	brought	(has) brought
drink	drank	(has) drunk
drive	drove	(has) driven
eat	ate	(has) eaten
give	gave	(has) given
go	went	(has) gone
lay	laid	(has) laid
lie	lay	(has) lain
rise	rose	(has) risen
say	said	(has) said
set	set	(has) set
sit	sat	(has) sat
speak	spoke	(has) spoken
swim	swam	(has) swum
teach	taught	(has) taught
write	wrote	(has) written

Of course, there are many more irregular verbs than these. To verify the correct past or past participle form of any irregular verb, consult a dictionary.

ACTIVITY 1

On the blank in each sentence, write the correct form of the verb in parentheses. Use the table above or a dictionary if you need help.

> **Samples:**
>
> **a.** I am late because I _____rode_____ the bus past the correct stop. *(ride)*
>
> **b.** How many times have you _____flown_____ on an airplane? *(fly)*

1. Unfortunately, when I _____ the baseball, it crashed through Mr. Rice's window. *(throw)*

2. Maleeka has _____ studying for the physics test already. *(begin)*

3. By 8:15 A.M., Mom had _____ my two brothers and me to three different schools. *(drive)*

4. Oscar bumped into a fragile vase, but he _____ it before it could hit the ground and break. *(catch)*

5. Marc was so tired after the basketball game on Saturday afternoon that he _____ on the sofa for an hour, napping. *(lie)*

6. As they crossed the busy street, Leyla _____ her little cousin's hand. *(hold)*

7. While learning to use in-line skates, I must have _____ a dozen times. *(fall)*

8. Who _____ my lunch sack from the refrigerator? *(take)*

9. Daphne said, "I _____ not take your lunch sack." *(do)*

10. Tariq had never _____ the song before, but his impromptu performance was fabulous. *(sing)*

ACTIVITY 2

Revise the following sentences to correct errors in verb forms. Cross out each incorrect verb and write the correct form above it. If you need help, consult a dictionary. The first sentence is completed as a sample. You should find seven additional errors.

As the U.S. population ~~growed~~ *grew* in the nineteenth century, the government tracked the numbers of immigrants who had ~~arrive~~ *arrived* from around the world. Many were Asians who seeked work. In their homelands, they had hear tales of wonderful opportunities in the West.

The government want a system of managing immigration. In 1894, Congress created the Bureau of Immigration. For over a century, immigrants from around the world had pour into the United States. Congress had pass the Chinese Exclusion Act in 1882. It ban the immigration of Chinese laborers into the States. However, immigrants still comed in great numbers. The Bureau of Immigration was formed to manage—and control—the influx of foreigners.

Using the Correct Forms of Verbs

Write your name at the top of a sheet of paper. Then write a sentence (on any topic) using the **past tense form** of one of these verbs: *become, break, choose, draw, fall, give, go, know, see, shake, swim, win.* (Consult a dictionary if you need help.) In your sentence, underline the verb.

With your teacher's approval, pass the paper to the person sitting behind you. Look at the underlined verb in the sentence you receive and write a new sentence (on any topic) using the **past participle form** of that verb. Underline the verb. Finally, write a new sentence using the **past tense form** of a different verb from the list.

Continue this process until you have written **ten** different sentences. Retrieve the paper with your name on it and read what others have written. Check to make sure they used the correct forms of verbs in the sentences. Correct any errors you find.

2. Does the verb in each sentence agree with its subject?

A subject and its verb must agree in number. This means that a plural subject takes a plural verb, and a singular subject takes a singular verb.

SINGULAR: An *immigrant comes* to the United States for a particular reason.

SINGULAR: *Work is* one reason.

PLURAL: *Immigrants come* to the United States for particular reasons.

PLURAL: *Jobs are* important to these newcomers.

Words or phrases that come between the subject and its verb do not affect subject-verb agreement (except in the case of a few indefinite pronouns—more on that in a moment).

SINGULAR: An *immigrant* from one of the Eastern countries *travels* a great distance to America.

(The singular verb *travels* agrees with the singular subject *immigrant.* The prepositional phrases do not affect subject-verb agreement.)

SINGULAR: The *person* who leaves behind family members *risks* loneliness.

(The singular verb *risks* agrees with the singular subject *person.* The clause between subject and verb does not affect subject-verb agreement.)

PLURAL: *Immigrants* from Asia *include* Chinese, Vietnamese, Thai, and others.

(The plural verb *include* agrees with the plural subject *Immigrants.*)

PLURAL: *People* who leave behind a family *feel* lonely.

(The plural verb *feel* agrees with the plural subject *people.*)

The indefinite pronouns *each, either, one, everybody, anyone,* and *anybody* are singular. They take singular verbs.

SINGULAR: *Everybody desires* a better life.

SINGULAR: *Each* of the immigrants *wants* a better life.

The indefinite pronouns *all, any, some, none, half,* and *most* may be singular or plural, depending on the sentence.

PLURAL: *All* of the immigrants *have* visas.

(Compare to *All immigrants have visas.*)

SINGULAR: *All* of the work *has been* difficult.

(Compare to *All work has been difficult.*)

PLURAL: *None* of the visas *were* for children.

(The prepositional phrase *of the visas* modifies the subject *None.* The plural object *visas* is the clue that the verb *were* should be plural.)

SINGULAR: *None* of the procedure *was* complete.

(The prepositional phrase *of the procedure* modifies the subject *None.* The singular object *procedure* is the clue that the verb *was* should be singular. *None* in this example means "no part of.")

ACTIVITY 3

Revise the following sentences to correct errors in subject-verb agreement. First, underline the subject once and the verb twice. Then cross out each incorrect verb and write the correct form above it. If a sentence needs no change, write *no change* on the blank.

has

Samples:

_____ **a.** One of the officials ~~have~~ my work visa.

____*no change*____ **b.** Any of the officials <u>are</u> available to help you.

_____ **1.** Each of these students are in the foreign exchange program.

_____ **2.** Some of my friends have student visas.

_____ **3.** Yes, all of those people are tourists.

_____ **4.** Everybody in the group carry a tourist visa.

_____ **5.** Half of my relatives are from Poland.

_____ **6.** One of my relatives have returned to Poland to visit.

_____ **7.** Truthfully, none of the country seems familiar to me.

_____ **8.** Most of my life has been spent in the United States.

_____ **9.** In my opinion, either of these embassies are a good place to work.

_____ **10.** Most of the employees at the embassy speaks two languages.

3. Is the verb tense consistent from sentence to sentence?

As you know, the *tense* of a verb shows the time of the action or the state of being that the verb expresses. Study the following examples of the six main verb tenses:

PRESENT TENSE: The Statue of Liberty *stands* on Ellis Island.

                      (The action occurs in the present or is habitually true.)

PAST TENSE: Harriet Tubman *started* the Underground Railroad.

                      (The action occurred in the past.)

FUTURE TENSE: Some baseball cards *will become* valuable over time.

                      (The action will occur at some time in the future.)

PRESENT PERFECT TENSE: Scientists *have placed* a robot on Mars.

                      (The action is completed in the present time. The use of present perfect tense emphasizes the relevance of the action to the current time.)

PAST PERFECT TENSE: By the 1950s, watching television *had become* an American pastime.

                      (The action was completed before a specific time in the past.)

FUTURE PERFECT TENSE: By 2040, television *will have celebrated* its 100th birthday.

                      (The action will be completed before a specific time in the future.)

Notice that the perfect tenses always use a form of *have* (*have, has,* or *had*). The future tenses always use *will*.

In a piece of writing, use the same verb tense in all sentences unless you have a specific reason for changing tenses. Study the examples below (sentences have been numbered for the sake of discussion).

CONSISTENT TENSE: [1]In college, Josh *took* classes in education. [2]Specifically, he *wanted* to teach English as a foreign language. [3]After he *graduated*, he *took* a job in Japan. [4]There, he *teaches* English to business professionals.	The actions in sentences 1–3 all take place in the past, so all the verbs are in past tense. In sentence 4, the action is a habitual action in the present, so *teaches* is correct in the present tense.
CONSISTENT TENSE: [1]In Japan, Josh *fell* in love with Nariko, a lovely woman. [2]They *dated* for a year, and then Josh *proposed* marriage. [3]Right now, they *are planning* two weddings. [4]One *will be* in Japan, and one *will be* in Michigan.	The action in sentences 1 and 2 happened in the past, so verbs are in past tense. The action in sentence 3 is ongoing in the present, so *are planning* is correct. All action in sentence 4 will take place in the future, so *will be* is correct.

In each example above, there are at least two different verb tenses. However, there is a logical reason for each change in tense. The important thing to remember is that there must be a valid reason for changing tenses within a set of related sentences.

Revise the sentences in the following passage to create consistent verb tense. Cross out each incorrect verb and write the correct form above it. The first sentence is completed as a sample. You should correct seven errors.

After the Bureau of Immigration formed, more restrictions ~~are~~ *were* passed. For example, in 1902 the immigration of Asians from Hawaii, the Philippines, and other U.S. island territories was being prohibited.

In the 1920s, Congress curbs immigration again. Specifically, the Emergency Quota Act of 1921 restricted immigration to 3 percent of the number of U.S. residents of that nationality. The numbers used for reference are gathered in 1910. In 1924, Congress again limits immigration, but mainly that of Asians. Canadians and Latin Americans were not limited, and they are immigrating in great numbers.

Finally, in 1965, a new act set overall limits for visas. Visas from the Western Hemisphere are limited to 120,000 per year. Visas from elsewhere in the world were limited to 170,000 per year. Relatives of U.S. citizens will not be counted toward these totals.

Modifiers

As you know, the job of a modifier is to modify, or describe, a part of speech in a sentence. In particular, *adjectives* modify nouns and pronouns. *Adverbs* modify verbs, adjectives, and adverbs. A modifier may take the form of a word, a phrase, or a clause. Whatever form it takes, a modifier functions as a single part of speech (adjective or adverb).

To verify that you have used modifiers correctly in your sentences, ask yourself a few simple questions.

1. Is the modifier in the correct form?

Be sure that you use an adjective form to modify a noun or pronoun. Use an adverb form to modify a verb, an adjective, or an adverb. Most writers have more trouble with adverbs than with adjectives.

ADJECTIVES: Nariko's English is *good*. (NOT *well*)

(*Good* follows the linking verb *is* and modifies the noun *English*.)

The application process can be *slow*. (NOT *slowly*)

(*Slow* follows the linking verb *can be* and modifies the noun *process*.)

ADVERBS: Nariko speaks English *well*. (NOT *good*)

(*Well* modifies the verb *speaks*.)

The application process can move *really slowly*. (NOT *real slow*)

(*Really* modifies the adverb *slowly*, and *slowly* modifies the verb *can move*.)

Nariko learned English *quickly*. (NOT *quick*)

(*Quickly* modifies the verb *learned*.)

ACTIVITY 5 _____

In the following passage, correct modifiers that are in the wrong form. Cross out each incorrect modifier and write the correct form above it. The first sentence is completed as a sample. You should correct seven errors.

Nariko has always been ~~well~~ *good* with languages. She studies a language real careful, and

she picks it up fast.

Her native language is Japanese, which she speaks fluent. When she began studying

English, this Western language seemed difficult. However, she was real patient, and soon

she began speaking English more skillfully. After a full year of intensely study, she spoke

English with only a slightly accent. Besides speaking good English, she speaks German

perfect.

2. Does the placement of the modifier create ambiguity?

A modifier placed too far from the word or word group it modifies can seem to modify the wrong word. Confusion or multiple meanings may result. Make sure each modifier is as close as possible to the word it modifies.

MISPLACED: Textbooks are priced at twenty dollars *for this class*.

(*For this class* seems to modify *dollars*. Is the twenty-dollar price just for this class? Or is the phrase supposed to modify *Textbooks*?)

CLEAR: Textbooks *for this class* are priced at twenty dollars.

(*For this class* clearly modifies *Textbooks*.)

MISPLACED: The research materials were written in Japanese *that Nariko used*.

(The clause *that Nariko used* seems to modify *Japanese*.)

CLEAR: The research materials *that Nariko used* were written in Japanese.

(Now the clause clearly and logically modifies *materials*.)

3. Does the modifier clearly describe a word or word group in the sentence?

Each modifier should logically modify a specific word or word group in its sentence. When a modifier does not logically modify a word in the sentence, we say that it is dangling.

DANGLING: *Flipping to the third chapter,* the past tense verbs looked difficult.

(*Flipping to the third chapter* does not logically modify any word in the sentence.)

CLEAR: *Flipping to the third chapter,* Nariko decided that the past tense verbs looked difficult.

(Now the phrase logically modifies *Nariko.* This revision required the addition of a noun, verb, and relative pronoun: *Nariko decided that.*)

DANGLING: *Printed in boldface,* students studied carefully.

(*Printed in boldface* does not logically modify any word in the sentence.)

CLEAR: Students carefully studied the key words, *printed in boldface.*

(Now the phrase logically modifies *words.* Also, the adverb *carefully* is next to the verb *studied.*)

ACTIVITY 6

Revise each sentence to correct errors in modifiers. To correct a word or two, cross out the incorrect words and write the correct words above them. To make extensive changes, write the revised sentence on the lines provided.

> **Samples:**
>
> a. English verbs ~~in the book~~ are the subject of the first three chapters ⟨in the book⟩.
>
> _____
>
> _____
>
> b. Written in English, some new immigrants aren't sure of the meaning.
>
> *Written in English, road signs are meaningless to some new immigrants.*
>
> *Here is an alternate revision of sample b:*
>
> *Some new immigrants aren't sure of the meanings of road signs written in English.*

1. Looking for tax information, the IRS Web site is available to workers.

_____

_____

2. A hot link provides access to a Web site in Spanish on the home page.

_____

_____

3. Printed in their native language, Spanish speakers are sure to understand.

_____

_____

4. Telephone menus are recorded in different languages, willing to help nonnative speakers.

_____

_____

5. After dialing the telephone number, option 1 accesses an English menu, and option 2 is _para Español._

_____

_____

6. Voter registration forms are a big help that are translated into Spanish.

_____

_____

7. Many popular movies are available with Spanish subtitles that are on DVD.

_____

_____

8. Viewers can read the subtitles who are unsure of the English.

_____

_____

9. Reading Spanish subtitles, they help English speakers learn Spanish.

_____

_____

10. Truly bilingual, opportunities in the job market are numerous.

_____

_____

Pronouns

To make sure your sentences use pronouns correctly, ask yourself these two questions:

1. Does the pronoun agree with its antecedent?

A pronoun must agree with its antecedent in _number_ (singular or plural) and in _gender_ (male, female, or neuter). As you may recall, the _antecedent_ is the noun or pronoun for which a pronoun stands. In the following examples, the pronouns and their antecedents are in bold type.

SINGULAR, MALE:	*Josh* lived in Japan three years while *he* taught English.

SINGULAR, FEMALE:	*Nariko* met Josh at the school where *she* taught computer classes.

SINGULAR, NEUTER:	The *school* has a beautiful fountain in front of *it*.

The plural pronouns indicate number but not gender.

PLURAL:	*Waves* in the water reflected sunlight from *their* surfaces.

PLURAL:	*Josh and Nariko* met when *they* both sat down near the fountain.

Composition Hint

Using a masculine pronoun to refer to an antecedent that could mean a man or a woman is a practice based on outdated rules. Nowadays, many people consider this to be *sexist language,* but you can avoid this problem.

INSTEAD OF:	Each *student* should write *his* name on the test booklet.

WRITE:	Each *student* should write *his or her* name on the test booklet.

Do not try to fix the problem by using *their* to refer to a singular antecedent. This usage is incorrect grammar.

INSTEAD OF:	Each *student* should write *their* name on the test booklet.

WRITE:	*Students* should write *their* names on the test booklets.

2. Does the pronoun refer clearly to a specific antecedent?

Make sure that the antecedent of each pronoun is clear. If you are in doubt, use a noun instead of a pronoun. In the example below, the sentences are numbered for the sake of discussion.

[1]When Nariko was twenty-four years old, *she* was teaching computer classes at a small school near Tokyo. [2]*It* was a fabulous place. [3]*She* had been dating a boyfriend from college, but *their* relationship wasn't good. [4]Then she met Josh. [5]*She* knew *she* must have a serious talk with *him*.	In this passage, most pronouns have clear antecedents. In sentence 1, the antecedent of *she* is *Nariko*. Since no other female is mentioned in the passage, *Nariko* is the clear antecedent of each *she*. In sentence 3, the plural pronoun *their* clearly refers to *she* and *boyfriend*. The antecedent of *It* in sentence 2 is unclear. Is it *school* or *Tokyo*? The antecedent of *him* in sentence 5 is unclear. Is it *boyfriend* or *Josh*?

Correct the pronoun errors in the following passage. Cross out incorrect words and write the correct words above them. The first sentence is completed as a sample. You should correct thirteen errors.

her
Nariko wanted to introduce Josh to ~~their~~ mom and dad. At this time, they lived in a tiny house on the edge of the city. She warned her parents that their new boyfriend was not Japanese. Her dad had always hoped she would marry a fine Japanese man. Josh, however, was American. Nariko wasn't sure if he would accept him.

She met at a sushi restaurant near their house. They were pleased when Josh eagerly consumed the raw fish on its plate. Besides that, her mom could clearly see that Josh cared deeply for her. She knew that Josh was making a good impression. Not only that, but he showed great respect to him, which was important to it. Overall, the meal was enjoyable to all of them.

Other Errors

Besides the grammar errors discussed already in this lesson, a few others deserve mention. Avoid the following:

1. Ending a sentence with a preposition

In general, do not end a sentence with a preposition. Doing so separates the preposition from its object.

INSTEAD OF THIS:	Where did you get that Spanish book *from*?
WRITE THIS:	*From* where did you get that Spanish book?
OR THIS:	Where did you get that Spanish book? (no preposition)
INSTEAD OF THIS:	I need a pencil to take my test *with*.
WRITE THIS:	I need a pencil *with* which to take my test.
OR THIS:	I need a pencil to use *during* my test. (different preposition)

In some cases, writers need to end a sentence with a preposition to achieve a specific effect. Notice the difference in the meanings of the following sentences:

1. Teaching English is what Josh is good at. (emphasizes Teaching English)

2. Josh is good at teaching English. (emphasizes *Josh*)

2. Splitting an infinitive

As you recall, an infinitive is *to* plus the base form of a verb. Infinitives are used as nouns, adjectives, or adverbs in sentences. In general, avoid placing words between *to* and the verb of an infinitive.

SPLIT INFINITIVE:	Nariko wants *to carefully control* the wedding costs.
CORRECT:	Nariko wants *to control* the wedding costs carefully.
SPLIT INFINITIVE:	*To routinely save* money, Josh quit buying fast food.
CORRECT:	*To save* money routinely, Josh quit buying fast food.

Occasionally, writers need to split an infinitive in order to best express a thought. Which of the following sentences seems stronger to you?

1. To truly understand English, you must know the verbs.

2. To understand English truly, you must know the verbs.

Most likely, you chose sentence 1. The modifier *truly* is most effective when placed just before *understand* instead of after *English.* Most of the time, however, writers can express ideas precisely without breaking rules of grammar.

3. Using a double negative

A *negative* is a "no" word such as *no, not, none, never, nobody, nothing, hardly,* or *scarcely.* The *n't* in a contraction (such as *don't*) is a negative, too. A *double negative* occurs when *two* negatives are mistakenly used to make one negative statement.

DOUBLE NEGATIVE:	It was an accident; George *never* meant *nobody* any harm.
CORRECT:	It was an accident; George *never* meant *anybody* any harm.
CORRECT:	It was an accident; George meant *nobody* any harm.
DOUBLE NEGATIVE:	*None* of us heard *nothing* about who stole the school mascot.
CORRECT:	*None* of us heard *anything* about who stole the school mascot.
CORRECT:	We heard *nothing* about who stole the school mascot.

ACTIVITY 8 _____

In the following passage, correct errors in the placement of prepositions, split infinitives, and double negatives. Cross out words and write corrections above them. The first two sentences are completed as samples. You should make five corrections.

Nariko had always wanted to ~~one day~~ visit America ^one day^. This large country had always

seemed an exciting place to ^visit^ ~~go to~~. In New York City, there were museums filled with art to

marvel at. On the coasts were hot, sandy beaches; the sand was the perfect kind to happily

build sand castles with. Native American culture was what the southwestern states were

influenced by. To actually walk through an ancient Anasazi village would be such a thrill.

Nariko and Josh thought about what their options were. After getting married, they could

live either in Japan or the United States. They could hardly decide which country they wanted

to permanently live in. However, Nariko was thrilled with one decision. They were planning to

definitely spend their honeymoon in the States.

Errors in Mechanics

The *mechanics* of writing include punctuation, capitalization, and spelling. These technical aspects, along with good grammar, help writers compose clear, strong sentences. In this lesson, detailed tables provide handy summaries of key rules of mechanics. Using these tables, you can improve your ability to write strong sentences.

Punctuation

By signaling pauses, stops, quotations, important ideas, ownership, missing letters, titles, and so on, punctuation marks serve as road signs for readers of sentences. As a writer, you can help readers understand your ideas precisely by using punctuation correctly. To avoid the most common errors, master the following rules of usage.

PUNCTUATION MARK	WHAT IT DOES	EXAMPLES
comma (,)	With a conjunction, it joins sentences.	The Greeks were mighty warriors, *and* their champion was Achilles. Achilles was a magnificent warrior, *but* he had one weak spot.
	It separates items in a series.	Ancient stories feature *people*, *animals*, and *supernatural creatures*. These tales are set *in forests*, *under the sea*, *on mountains*, and *inside palaces*.
	It sets off introductory words and words groups, and sets off interrupting words and expressions.	In one classical myth, Atlas carries the world on his shoulders. The Greek and Roman myths, *in fact*, are popular with modern readers.
semicolon (;)	It joins sentences.	Circe was a sorceress; she turned men into swine. (no conjunction) Icarus flew with wax wings; *however*, they melted near the sun. (conjunctive adverb)
	It joins items in a series when one or more items have a comma.	Myths tell about Androcles, a slave; Cassandra, a prophet; and Atlas, a giant.
colon (:)	It calls attention to what follows.	Remember this: Even gods are not perfect. Achilles had one weak spot: his heel. The three Graces are these: Aglaia, Euphrosyne, and Thalia.

PUNCTUATION MARK	WHAT IT DOES	EXAMPLES
apostrophe (')	With *s*, it forms the possessive of singular words and of plurals not ending in *s*.	SINGULAR: warrior's sword, story's theme, lion's paw, goddess's temple PLURAL: children's stories, men's battles, women's interests
	It forms the possessive of plural words ending in *s*.	Trojans' horse, warriors' swords, stories' themes, goddesses' temples
	It forms contractions.	haven't, I've, they'll, we're
quotation marks (". . .")	A pair of them encloses direct quotations.	Daedalus said, "Do not fly near the sun." "I won't, Dad," said Icarus.
	A pair of them encloses the titles of short works.	"The Trojan Horse" (story), "Ballad of Dido" (song), "Ancient Greece" (article)
italics (or <u>underlining</u>)	They punctuate the titles of longer works.	*Mythology* (book), *Troy* (movie), <u>Travel and Leisure</u> (magazine), <u>Chicago Tribune</u> (newspaper)

ACTIVITY 1

Insert commas, semicolons, colons, and apostrophes where they are needed in the following passage. The first two sentences are completed as samples. You should make 15 insertions.

A myth's appeal lies in two main elements: characters and plot. For example, one myth tells of a conceited man; he is punished for this flaw. The storys main character is Narcissus and he attracted the gods disapproval.

This young mans eyes were large dark and mysterious his hair was shiny and curly and his face glowed with health. His problem was this being obsessed with his own beauty. One fine day he was admiring his reflection in a pool of water and he couldnt pull himself away. As a matter of fact he stared and stared. To teach Narcissus a lesson the gods turned him into a narcissus (a type of flower). In modern times a person who is in love with his or her own self is called narcissistic.

ACTIVITY 2

Punctuate each title correctly by adding quotation marks or underlining. A clue in parenthesis helps you determine whether the title is that of a short work or a longer work.

1. King Arthur (movie)

2. Pandora's Forbidden Box (short story)

3. The Lady of Shalott (poem)

4. The Mammoth Book of Myths (book)

5. West Hartford News (newspaper)

6. Forgive Me, Antigone (song)

7. Death of a Salesman (play)

8. Was King Arthur Real? (article)

9. Anthology of World Literature (book)

10. Psychology Today (magazine)

QUESTION: How do I use quotation marks with other punctuation marks?

ANSWER: Follow these two guidelines:

(a) A period or a comma goes inside a closing quotation mark.

Mr. Valdez said, "Athena was the goddess of wisdom."

"The goddess of wisdom," said Mr. Valdez, "was Athena."

(b) An exclamation point or question mark goes inside the closing quotation mark if it is part of the direct quotation. Otherwise, it goes outside.

"Why shouldn't I open the box?" asked Pandora.

(The quoted words ask a question, so the question mark is inside the quotation mark.)

When did Sir Walter Scott write "Lady of the Lake"?

(The entire sentence, not the quoted words, asks a question, so the question mark is outside the quotation mark.)

ACTIVITY 3

Insert quotation marks exactly where they are needed in the following passage. The first paragraph is completed as a sample.

The Oracle at Delphi spoke to Oedipus. "One day," said the oracle (prophet), "you will kill

your father and marry your mother."

I don't believe it, said Oedipus. But just to be sure, I will travel far away. And Oedipus did not go home to the palace where he had been raised by the king and queen of Corinth.

Oedipus set out on a journey, though he had no particular destination. One day, he encountered a belligerent old man who hogged the narrow road.

Let me pass! demanded Oedipus.

Do you dare tell me what to do? said the older man in fury. You let me pass.

The argument turned nasty; they brawled; Oedipus killed the stranger. In a huff, he traveled on, finally coming to the city of Thebes. There, he met Jocasta the queen, who was a widow.

One day, Oedipus said to Jocasta, I love you. Marry me.

My love, of course I will marry you! she replied. We will rule Thebes together.

The wedding took place. Little did Oedipus know that by killing the old man on the road and by marrying Jocasta, he had killed his father and married his mother—who had given him up for adoption at his birth.

Capitalization

The guidelines in the following table tell what kinds of words to capitalize.

CAPITALIZE . . .	EXAMPLES
the first word in a sentence.	**A** giant with one eye in its forehead is a Cyclops.
the pronoun *I*.	In the library, **I** found a book about King Midas.
the first word in a direct quotation.	Ms. Kuo said, "**Please** research the Trojan War."
proper nouns, their abbreviations,	John **Smith**, **Ms. Kuo**, **King Midas**, **Greece**
and proper adjectives.	**Oct.**, **Mr.**, **Dr.**, **Prof.**, **Ave.**, **St.**, **Corp.**, **Inc.** **Trojan**, **Greek**, **Mediterranean**, **American**
the first and all main words in titles.	"**The Winged Horse**" (story) *The Golden Touch of Midas* (book) *The Mysts of Avalon* (movie)
the first word and all nouns in the salutation, and the first word in the closing of a letter.	**Dear Professor Abrams:** **Sincerely** yours,
the names of specific regions	the **Northeast**, the **West**, the **Southwest**
words used as a name	**Mom**, **Dad**, **Cousin Tristan** (but NOT *my Mom, your Dad, our Cousin*)

For guidelines on spelling abbreviations, including initials, turn to the table on page 87.

ACTIVITY 4

Correct errors in capitalization. Cross out each lowercase letter that should be a capital, and write the capital letter above it. Cross out capital letters that should be lowercase, and write the lowercase letter above. The first sentence is completed as a sample. You should make 26 corrections. (In *Le morte d'arthur*, the *d* should not be capitalized.)

M̶rs. r̶eilly began C̶lass by saying, "g̶reek and r̶oman myths are filled with supernatural beings, but so are other types of L̶iterature. who has read about supernatural Creatures living beneath the surface of a Lake?"

Looking around the classroom, i saw my twin Sister, penelope, raise her hand. She said, "I saw *Scooby-Doo and the loch ness monster*." Everyone laughed. Mentally, i filed her comment away to tell mom.

Mrs. reilly grimaced. "okay," she said. "that's a start. but let me tell you about a literary character who lived in a Lake. She is called the lady of the lake, and she shows up in a long Work by sir thomas Malory called *Le morte d'arthur*. This lake lady gives the famous sword, excalibur, to arthur."

Spelling

Use the following rules to avoid common spelling mistakes.

Helpful Spelling Rules

RULE	EXAMPLES
Write *i* before *e* except after *c,* or when sounded like *a* as in *neighbor* and *weigh*.	n**ie**ce, ch**ie**f, f**ie**ld, ach**ie**ve conc**ei**t, rec**ei**pt, c**ei**ling, rec**ei**ve
When adding a **prefix**, do not change the spelling of the original word.	co + operate = cooperate non + sense = nonsense semi + circle = semicircle
When adding the **suffix *ly*** or ***ness***, do not change the spelling of the original word. *Exception:* Words ending in a consonant and *y*. See rule on following page.	legal + ly = legal**ly** neat + ly = neat**ly** great + ness = great**ness** glad + ness = glad**ness**

RULE	EXAMPLES
When a word ends in a **consonant and y**, change the *y* to *i* before a suffix not beginning with *i*.	hairy + ness = hair**i**ness funny + ness = funn**i**ness fly + ing = fl**y**ing
When a word ends in a **vowel and y**, keep the *y* when adding a suffix.	terrify + ing = terrif**y**ing joy + ous = jo**y**ous
When a word ends in a **silent e** . . . . . . drop the *e* to add a suffix beginning with a vowel. . . . keep the *e* to add a suffix beginning with a consonant.	skate + ing = skat**ing** write + er = writ**er** amaze + ment = amaz**ement** hope + ful = hop**eful**
Double the final consonant before a suffix beginning with a vowel if the word is one syllable or is accented on the final syllable.	snug + er = snu**gg**er snap + y = sna**pp**y unplug + ing = unplu**gg**ing
Do not double the consonant if it is preceded by more than one vowel.	clean + est = clean**est** sleep + er = slee**per**

ACTIVITY 5

Follow the instructions to spell new words and write them on the lines provided.

Samples:

a. Add *op* to *press*. _____*oppress*_____

b. Add *ist* to *elite*. _____*elitist*_____

1. Add *co* to *education*. _____

2. Add *ible* to *reverse*. _____

3. Add *en* to *loose*. _____

4. Add *ly* to *natural*. _____

5. Add *un* to *natural*. _____

6. Add *ty* to *safe*. _____

7. Add *less* to *name*. _____

8. Add *ness* to *friendly*. _____

9. Add *ing* to *cry*. _____

10. Add *y* to *bag*. _____

Another set of rules govern the spelling of plural nouns. The rules below will help you avoid the most common spelling mistakes. Notice that an apostrophe is *never* used to make a noun plural (three *buses,* NOT three *bus's*).

Spelling the Plurals of Nouns

SPELLING RULE	EXAMPLES
For **most nouns**, add *s* to the singular to form the plural.	raisin**s**, shoestring**s**, motor**s**, note**s**, message**s**, computer**s**, snack**s**
For **nouns ending in *s, sh, ch,*** or ***x,*** add *es* to form the plural.	pass**es**, crash**es**, patch**es**, box**es**
For **most nouns ending in *f*,** change *f* to *v* and add *es* to form the plural. For a few nouns ending in *f*, add *s*.	leaf, lea**ves** thief, thie**ves** hoof, hoo**ves** roof, roof**s** belief, belief**s**
For three nouns ending in *fe*—***knife, life, wife***—change *f* to *v* and add *s* to form the plural.	knife, kni**ves** life, li**ves** wife, wi**ves**
For nouns ending in a **consonant plus *y*,** change the *y* to *i* and add *es*.	enemy, enem**ies** company, compan**ies**
For **nouns ending in *o*,** add *s* in most cases. For some nouns ending in a consonant plus *o*, add *es*.	video**s**, piano**s**, soprano**s**, memento**s**, radio**s** tomato/tomato**es**, potato/potato**es**
Some nouns form their plurals **irregularly**.	child, children crisis, crises datum, data deer, deer foot, feet goose, geese louse, lice man, men medium, media moose, moose mouse, mice ox, oxen parenthesis, parentheses series, series sheep, sheep shrimp, shrimp syllabus, syllabi thesis, theses tooth, teeth woman, women

ACTIVITY 6 _____

Write the plural of each noun.

Samples:

a. sphere _____ *spheres* _____

b. wolf _____ *wolves* _____

1. shoe _____

2. branch _____

3. astronaut _____

4. berry _____

5. alto _____

6. life _____

7. belief _____

8. duplex _____

9. helicopter _____

10. woman _____

Certain words in the English language tend to confuse writers, not because of their spellings but because of their meanings. We sometimes write *accept* when we mean *except*, or *they're* when we mean *there*. The following list includes many of these often-confused words, along with brief definitions. Many of these words have multiple meanings, though some meanings are rarely used. The most common meanings are explained below.

Anytime you are unsure of the spelling or the meaning of a word, consult a dictionary.

aisle, isle	*aisle:* walkway between sections of seats
	isle: island
accept, except	*accept:* to receive willingly
	except: to exclude
affect, effect	*affect:* to produce a result upon
	effect: (*n.*) a result; (*v.*) to bring about a result
altar, alter	*altar:* a table used in a religious ritual or ceremony
	alter: to change
brake, break	*brake:* a device used to slow or stop movement
	break: a period of rest
capital, capitol	*capital:* a city that serves as a seat of government
	capitol: a building in which a legislative body meets
chose, choose	*chose:* past tense of the verb *choose*, meaning "to select"
	choose: to select
coarse, course	*coarse:* rough; made of large particles
	course: the path over which something moves; a plan of study
complement, compliment	*complement:* to complete or go well with
	compliment: to give a flattering remark
council, counsel	*council:* an organized body of people
	counsel: advice
desert, dessert	*desert:* (*n.*) a dry, hot, sandy region; (*v.*) to leave behind
	dessert: a sweet food

its, it's	*its:* the possessive form of the pronoun *it*
	it's: contraction of *it is*
loose, lose	*loose:* not tight
	lose: to miss from one's possession; to fail to win
principal, principle	*principal:* (*adj.*) most important; (*n.*) person in charge of a school
	principle: a law, rule, or code of conduct
than, then	*than:* a term used to form comparisons, as in *taller than you*
	then: a point in time
their, there, they're	*their:* possessive form of the pronoun *they*
	there: a designation of a location
	they're: contraction of *they are*
to, too, two	*to:* preposition used to relate its object to another word in the sentence
	too: also; in addition
	two: numerical indication of one plus one
weather, whether	*weather:* conditions of rain, snow, sun, temperature, etc.
	whether: used to link alternatives, as in *whether you heard me or not;* used to express indirect questions, as in *I wonder whether you heard me*
wear, where	*wear:* to attire oneself with
	where: indication of direction or place
your, you're	*your:* possessive form of the pronoun *you*
	you're: contraction of *you are*

 Writing
Application

Using Often-Confused Words Correctly

Write your name at the top of a sheet of paper. Then choose one of the words in the list above that tends to give you trouble. Use the word to write a complete sentence, and underline the word in the sentence. With your teacher's approval, pass your paper to the person sitting behind you.

Read the sentence you receive. If the person used the underlined word correctly, write a check mark in the margin next to the sentence. If the word is used incorrectly, write the correct word above the error.

Then choose a new word from the list above and write a new sentence, passing it to the person behind you when you're finished. Continue with this process until you have written and checked **five** sentences. Retrieve the paper with your name on it and study the sentences that have been written. Check for correct usage of the underlined words and correct any errors you find.

Spelling Abbreviations and Numbers

Use the following helpful guidelines for spelling and using abbreviations and numbers.

GUIDELINE	EXAMPLES
Titles Place titles such as *Mr., Ms., Mrs., Dr.,* and *Prof.* before a proper name. Place designations such as *M.D.* and *Ph.D.* after a comma following the name.	*Mr.* Denzel Washington, *Ms.* Tyra Banks, *Dr.* Carl Sagan M. H. Abrams, *Ph.D.* Jonas Salk, *M.D.*
Streets, States, etc. In a sentence, do not abbreviate the names of streets, states, countries, continents, days of the week, months, or units of measure.	It happened on Lincoln *Street* near the deli. We'll study on *Monday* at the library. This steak weighs eight *ounces*.
Addresses In postal addresses, use proper abbreviations for states and street designations. For a complete list of abbreviations, go to the U.S. Postal Service's Web site (www.usps.com) and do a search for "abbreviations."	Drive = Dr. Road = Rd. Street = St. Boulevard = Blvd. California = CA Florida = FL Texas = TX New York = NY
Volume, Chapter, Page In sentences, write out the words *volume, chapter,* and *page.* When writing a source citation or bibliography, use the appropriate abbreviation (*vol.* or *vols., ch.* or *chs., p.* or *pp.*). *Note:* For exact format of citations and bibliographies, consult the style guide recommended by your teacher.	In Chapter Two, the author explains the results of her "splendiferous experiment" (Johnson, 2004, p. 56). Johnson, Nelda. *Experiments in Science.* Vol. 2. New York: Science House, 2004.
Initials Do not use periods with initials (*SAT, NATO, NASA, UNICEF, AIDS*). If your reader may not know what the initials stand for, spell out the words in the first instance of use, and place the initials in parentheses, as shown at right. Then use the initials after that.	Thousands of students will take the *SAT* this weekend. Opponents of the *North American Free Trade Agreement* (*NAFTA*) met yesterday in Chicago. Special speakers on *NAFTA* issues include Dr. Jerome Gerard.
Years When using *B.C.* or *A.D.* with a year, place *B.C.* after the year. Place *A.D.* before the year.	3500 B.C. A.D. 2005
Numbers When you use numbers in sentences, write out the number if it can be expressed in one or two words. Use figures for other numbers **unless** the number is the first word in a sentence. Always spell out a number that begins a sentence.	I invited *twenty-five* friends to the party, but only *seventeen* showed up. At the pet adoption event, *111* dogs and cats found loving homes. *One hundred eleven* dogs and cats found loving homes at the pet adoption event.

8 Review of Sentence Revision

Recall these serious—though fixable—errors in **grammar**:

- sentence fragment
- run-on sentence
- comma splice
- incorrect verb form
- lack of agreement between subject and verb
- inconsistent verb tense
- incorrect form of modifier (adverbs and adjectives)
- misplaced modifier
- dangling modifier
- lack of agreement between pronoun and antecedent
- pronoun with no clear antecedent
- double negative

ACTIVITY 1

Revise sentences in the following passage to correct fragments, run-ons, and comma splices. Cross out errors and write corrections above them. The first error is corrected as a sample. You should correct five errors.

Ancient Egyptians believed in a kind of life after death_x *i*n which a person existed in a manner similar to the life he or she had lived. For this reason, wealthy Egyptians filled the tombs of dead loved ones with a treasure trove of objects, they included exquisite furniture, lavish paintings, fabulous jewelry, golden dishes, and other items.

King Tut's tomb contained a wealth of royal possessions, among the carefully crafted furniture was the royal throne. Constructed of wood and elaborately carved in intricate patterns. Then it was overlaid with gold. Precious gems were set into the surface, two carved lion heads were set at the tops of the two front legs. The throne's backrest depicts the king, his queen, and the sun god showering light down upon them the throne dates to about 1340 B.C.

ACTIVITY 2

Revise sentences in the following passage to correct errors in verbs and modifiers. Cross out errors and write corrections above them. The first error is corrected as a sample. You should correct 15 errors.

Most—if not all—Americans ~~has~~ *have* heard of the Navajo, the Cherokee, the Sioux, and other native groups of North America. Surprisingly, many have never hear of one of the most ancient groups of all: the Anasazi. Modern-day descendants of the ancient group still live in the land of their ancestors, though not in the actually stone cities those ancestors builded. Tracing their roots to the prehistoric Basket Makers and Pueblo Indians, North America has been home to the Anasazi since about 5500 B.C. The name by which we knew them today, Anasazi, was gived them by the Navajo, which means Ancient Ones.

Today, ruins of Anasazi towns existing in southwestern Colorado, among other places. The Anasazi carved out small towns beginning in about A.D. 600 in the sides of cliffs. Living quarters was stacked rooms that actual resemble modern-day apartment buildings. "Doors" was holes in the floor accessed by climbing a ladder from the room below. In Colorado's Mesa Verde National Park, ruins in a cliff side is known as Mesa Verde. Walking inside the lower rooms, they are real sturdy and intact.

ACTIVITY 3 _____

Revise sentences in the following passage to correct errors in verbs and pronouns. Cross out errors and write corrections above them. The first error is corrected as a sample. You should correct 15 errors.

One of the most famous paintings in the world ~~are~~ ^{is} the *Mona Lisa.* Painted in oil in smoky, somber hues, he depicts a woman with a faint smile on its face. They look directly at the viewer. The artist who maked this (and other masterpieces) are Leonardo da Vinci. He complete it in 1506.

Leonardo becomed an artist as a teenager, when he beginned working for Andrea del Verrocchio as an apprentice. He lived and worked during a time of artistic rebirth called the Renaissance.

During the Renaissance, from the 14th to 17th centuries, art virtually exploding across Europe. The movement start first in Italy and then spreaded across the continent. Artists study art and ideas of ancient Greece and Rome. Using these classics as inspiration, he created amazing masterpieces in painting, sculpture, architecture, and other art forms.

Using Correct Grammar

On the Internet or in a book, find a photograph of a work of art that piques (grabs) your interest. Ask yourself a few questions about the piece. In what medium (paint, marble, wood, etc.) is the art? What colors did the artist use, and what mood do these colors create? (For example, the smoky hues in the *Mona Lisa* create a somber, even mysterious, mood.) What other detail of the art captures your attention?

Write **two** paragraphs of about **six to eight** sentences each, explaining your answers to the questions above. Be sure to identify the names of the artwork and its artist (or specify that the artists is unknown). Use the checklist on page 92 to edit your sentences for correct grammar.

Recall these common errors in **mechanics**:

- missing or misused comma (**,**)
- missing or misused semicolon (**;**)
- missing or misused colon (**:**)
- missing or misused apostrophe (**'**)
- missing quotation marks around direct quote ("...")
- missing quotation marks around title of short work ("...")
- missing *italics* or <u>underlining</u> for title of longer work
- missing or misused capital letter
- misspelled word
- misspelled plural of a noun

ACTIVITY 4

Revise sentences in the following passage to correct errors in the use of commas, semicolons, colons, and apostrophes. Add punctuation or cross it out, as needed. The first error is corrected as a sample. You should correct 19 errors.

Ancient Egyptians turned tombs into homes frozen in time; ancient Anasazi sculpted communities from rocky cliffs. These tombs and communities have something in common they are both kinds of art. Another kind of art is the mural which is a huge painting on the wall or side of a building or on a ceiling. For example Michelangelos lavish painting's on the ceiling of the Sistine Chapel are murals and Leonardo da Vincis famous *Last Supper* is a mural.

Murals arent limited to Renaissance artists like Michelangelo and Leonardo. Prehistoric cave paintings in France, and rock paintings in South Africa, can be seen as types of murals, in modern times, artists create murals on the walls' of schools shopping malls restaurants childrens rooms and more. Going to extremes some might even say that: graffiti covering a wall is a modern form of the mural. What do you think?

ACTIVITY 5

Revise sentences in the following passage to correct errors in quotation marks, capitalization, and spelling. Cross out errors and write corrections above them.

Hint: Web site *is capitalized correctly. The first three errors are corrected as samples. You should correct 37 errors.*

Today our new art␣t␣teacher arrived. Before school, ␣I␣had told ␣M␣mom, I realy miss mr. ustinov.

This new teacher better be good.

When ms. bassett walked into the room, I expected her too begin by takeing roll. instead, she began the lesson immediatly. She said, Let's talk about computer art. How many of you have ever scaned an image into a computer or used art software?

A few students, includeing me, raised there hands.

Ms. Bassett continued, One of my favorite computer artists is Barbara nessim. Have you heard of her? She paused, but no one raised a hand.

Nessim creates computer-generated image's as an art form, ms. Bassett sayed. "Some, like *modem: close encounter of the computer kind,* are enlarged to show individual pixels makeing up the image. Ms. Bassett opend a big book of art. She held up a page that showed the *Modem* image. She said, its great, isn't it?" Then she went on. "One of Nessim's favorite kinds of Art is what she calls the visual book. She creates visual novels and visual journals. You can see some examples online, right their on her Web site.

Writing Application

Sentence Revision

Do you think a wall covered in graffiti is a valid example of modern-day art? To develop your opinion, brainstorm at least three reasons it might be considered art and at least three reasons why it might not be considered art.

Use your prewriting to write a dialogue (written conversation) between two people who are arguing over whether graffiti is art. Write approximately one handwritten page in length. Use the checklist on page 92 to edit your sentences for correct use of punctuation, capitalization, and spelling.

Sentence Revision Checklist

Use this checklist as a guide when you write and revise sentences. It includes the characteristics of strong sentences (taught in Lessons 1–4) and problem areas in grammar and composition (taught in Lessons 5–8).

STYLE

Make sure your sentences are strong and forceful by including these stylistic qualities:

_____ conciseness

_____ clarity and specificity

_____ unity

_____ active voice unless there is a specific reason for passive voice

_____ sentence variety in length and structure

GRAMMAR

Proofread your sentences to correct grammar errors.

_____ sentence fragment

_____ run-on sentence

_____ comma splice

_____ incorrect verb form

_____ lack of agreement between subject and verb

_____ inconsistent verb tense

_____ incorrect form of modifier (adverbs and adjectives)

_____ misplaced modifier

_____ dangling modifier

_____ lack of agreement between pronoun and antecedent

_____ pronoun with no clear antecedent

_____ double negative

MECHANICS

Proofread your sentences to correct errors in mechanics.

_____ missing or misused comma (**,**)

_____ missing or misused semicolon (**;**)

_____ missing or misused colon (**:**)

_____ missing or misused apostrophe (**'**)

_____ missing quotation marks around direct quote ("...")

_____ missing quotation marks around title of short work ("...")

_____ missing *italics* or <u>underlining</u> for title of longer work

_____ missing or misused capital letter

_____ misspelled word

_____ misspelled plural of a noun

Sentence Revision

The following research applications encourage you to take your **sentence revision** beyond this workbook and into real life. Each assignment asks you to gather information on one of the themes in the previous lessons and to write and revise clear, forceful sentences about your findings. Enjoy your research and take pride in using your skills of sentence revision!

THEME: Technology

SKILL: Writing Complete, Correct Sentences

What piece of modern technology do you wish you owned? Imagine that you have the money to buy this item, whether it is a big-screen TV, a cell phone, a digital camera, or whatever. Do some research to determine which brand and model has the best customer satisfaction. To find reviews and ratings on the Internet, look on a merchant site or on a site such as ConsumerGuide (these offer free product reviews; ignore sites that ask you to subscribe to access reviews). In the library, look for product reviews in relevant magazines or in periodicals such as *Consumers Digest* and *Consumer Reports.*

After reading reviews and evaluating the pros and cons of various brands and models, select the exact item you would buy. Write **two** short paragraphs of about six sentences each or **one** long paragraph of about twelve sentences. Identify what piece of technology you would like to buy and explain why a particular brand and model is ideal for you. Use the Sentence Revision Checklist on pages 91–92 to check your sentences for completeness and correctness, making revisions as necessary.

THEME: International Travel

SKILL: Editing for Correct Grammar

For various reasons, many people seek work in a foreign country. If you were to do so, what kind of work would you seek? What country would you choose? How long would you stay? What benefits could you find in taking a job there instead of doing similar work in your home country?

To make an informed decision, research job opportunities in foreign countries. On the Internet, you can begin a search with the term "work abroad." In the library, you can find nonfiction books on individual countries, many with fabulous photographs.

Use your resources to develop answers to the questions above. Then write **two** paragraphs of **six to eight** sentences each. Explain what kind of work appeals to you, in what country, and why. Use the Sentence Revision Checklist on page 92 to check your sentences for errors in grammar, making revisions as necessary.

THEME: Mythology

SKILL: Editing for Correct Punctuation, Capitalization, and Spelling

Who was Pandora, and why was she not supposed to open a certain box? Why was Achilles' one physical weakness in his heel? Why did Daedalus make wax wings for his son? The answers to these questions may be found in classical mythology.

Choose a god or goddess mentioned in Lesson 7 or another mythological character of your choosing. Research the stories that are told about this character and write a summary of your findings. Write **two** paragraphs of around **six to eight** sentences each. Use the Sentence Revision Checklist on page 92 to check your sentences for correct punctuation, capitalization, and spelling. Make revisions as needed.

THEME: Art

SKILL: Editing for Correct Style, Grammar, and Mechanics

With your teacher's approval, choose a classmate with whom to work. Together, look at some of Barbara Nessim's computer art at www.nessim.com or www.barbaranessim.com. (Many school and public libraries have computers with Internet access available.) As you look at the art, discuss your opinions with your classmate and take notes on your discussion.

On your own, write a dialogue (written conversation) between two people, basing it on the discussion you had with your classmate regarding Nessim's art. Write approximately one handwritten page. Use the Sentence Revision Checklist on pages 91–92 to edit your sentences for correct use of style, grammar, and mechanics. Make revisions as necessary.

Sentence Revision

Directions: The sentence in each item may contain errors in grammar, punctuation, capitalization, and/or spelling. Circle the letter of the best revision of each sentence and write it on the blank. If the sentence is already correct, circle the letter for *NO CHANGE*.

_____ **1.** Frederick Douglass who was once a slave wrote "No man can put a chain about the ankle of his fellow man without at last finding the other end fastened about his own neck."

    A. NO CHANGE

    B. Frederick Douglass, who was once a slave, wrote, "No man can put a chain about the ankle of his fellow man without at last finding the other end fastened about his own neck."

    C. Frederick Douglass, who was once a slave wrote "No man can put a chain about the ankle of his fellow man without at last finding the other end fastened about his own neck."

    D. Frederick Douglass who was once a slave, wrote "No man can put a chain about the ankle of his fellow man without at last finding the other end fastened about his own neck."

_____ **2.** the inventor of the lightbulb, Thomas Edison, said, "Genius is one percent inspiration and ninety-nine percent perspiration."

    F. NO CHANGE

    G. The inventor of the lightbulb, Thomas Edison, said, Genius is one percent inspiration and ninety-nine percent perspiration.

    H. The inventor of the lightbulb, Thomas Edison, said, "Genius is one percent inspiration and ninety-nine percent perspiration."

    J. the inventor of the lightbulb, Thomas Edison, said, "Genius is one percent inspiration and ninety-nine percent perspiration".

_____ **3.** Another scientific genius, Albert Einstein, warned, "I don't know how the Third World War will be fought, but I do know how the Fourth will: with sticks and stones."

    A. NO CHANGE

    B. Another scientific genius, Albert Einstein, warned, i don't know how the Third World War will be fought, but I do know how the Fourth will: with sticks and stones.

    C. Another scientific genius Albert Einstein warned "I don't know how the Third World War will be fought, but I do know how the Fourth will with sticks and stones."

    D. Another scientific Genius, Albert Einstein, warned, "I don't know how the Third World War will be fighted, but I do know how the Fourth will; with sticks and stones."

_____ 4. the poet langston hughes wrote hold fast to dreams, for if dreams die, life is a broken-winged bird that cannot fly."

    F. NO CHANGE

    G. The poet Langston Hughes wrote, "Hold fast to dreams, for if dreams die, life is a broken-winged bird that cannot fly."

    H. The poet Langston Hughes wrote: "Hold fast to dreams, for if dreams die, life is a broken-winged bird that cannot fly."

    J. The Poet Langston Hughes wrote, "Hold fast to dreams, for if dreams die, life is a broken-winged bird that cannot fly".

_____ 5. In the song "Lift Ev'ry Voice and Sing" which many African Americans consider their national anthem James Weldon Johnson wrote, "Facing the rising sun of our new day begun let us march on till victory is won."

    A. NO CHANGE

    B. In the song "Lift Ev'ry Voice and Sing," which many African Americans consider their national anthem, James Weldon Johnson wrote, "Facing the rising sun of our new day begun let us march on till victory is won."

    C. In the song _Lift Ev'ry Voice and Sing,_ which many African Americans consider their national anthem, James Weldon Johnson wrote, "Facing the rising sun of our new day begun let us march on till victory is won."

    D. In the song "Lift Ev'ry Voice and Sing," which many African Americans consider their national anthem, James Weldon Johnson wrote, Facing the rising sun of our new day begun let us march on till victory is won.

_____ 6. Were it Jackie Robinson who said, "A life is not important except in the impact it has on other lifes"?

    F. NO CHANGE

    G. Was it Jackie Robinson who said, "A life is not important except in the impact it has on other lives"?

    H. Were it Jackie Robinson who said, "A life is not important except in the impact it has on other lives?"

    J. Was it Jackie Robinson who said, "A life is not important except in the impact it has on other lives."

_____ 7. Tecumseh was a warrior and leader in the Shawnee nation during the time that American colonists were sweeping westward, taking land from Native Americans.

    A. NO CHANGE

    B. Tecumseh was a warrior and leader in the shawnee nation during the time that american colonists were sweeping westward, taking land from native americans.

    C. Tecumseh was a warrior and leader in the Shawnee nation during the time that American colonyists was sweeping Westward, taking land from Native Americans.

    D. Tecumseh is a warrior and leader in the Shawnee nation during the time that American colonists are sweeping westward, takeing land from Native Americans.

_____ **8.** Tecumseh said Sell a country! Why not sell the air the clouds and the great sea as well as the earth did not the Great Spirit make them all for the use of his childs?

    F. NO CHANGE

    G. Tecumseh said, Sell a country! Why not sell the air, the clouds, and the great sea as well as the earth? Did not the Great Spirit make them all for the use of his children?

    H. Tecumseh said, "Sell a country! Why not sell the air, the clouds, and the great sea as well as the earth? Did not the Great Spirit make them all for the use of his children?"

    J. Tecumseh said, "Sell a country! Why not sell the air; the clouds; and the great sea; as well as the earth, did not the Great Spirit make them all for the use of his children?"

_____ **9.** Harriet Tubman is an abolitionist; he organized the Underground Railroad as a means of helping escaped slaves find they're way to the North.

    A. NO CHANGE

    B. Harriet Tubman was an abolitionist, she organized the underground railroad as a means of helping escaped slaves find their way to the north.

    C. Harriet Tubman was an abolitionist; she organized the Underground Railroad as a means of helping escaped slaves find their way to the North.

    D. Harriet Tubman is an abolitionist she organized the Underground Railroad as a means of helping escaped slaves find there way to the north.

_____ **10.** This freedom fighter said On my Underground Railroad, I never ran my train off the track, and I never lost a passenger.

    F. NO CHANGE

    G. This freedom fighter said, "On my Underground Railroad, I never runned my train of the track and I never lost a passenger."

    H. This freedom fighter said "On my Underground Railroad I never runned my train off the track, I never losed a passenger."

    J. This freedom fighter said, "On my Underground Railroad, I never ran my train off the track, and I never lost a passenger."

Directions: On the lines provided, rewrite each item, correcting errors in grammar, punctuation, and spelling.

11. Readers who are interested in Tubman's Underground Railroad. Can read about it in Passages to Freedom, a book by David W. Blight.

_____

_____

12. Speaking in support of migrant workers rights, peaceful protests and speeches were what Cesar Chavez did.

_____

_____

13. Chavez, working with Dolores Huerta. They established United Farm Worker's of America.

_____

_____

14. Rachel Carson, author of the book silent spring, was an environmental activist she lived from 1907 two 1964.

_____

_____

15. Sandra day o'Connor was the first woman justice of the u.s. supreme court.

_____

_____

16. Celebratd today for not giveing up its bus seat too a white man, Rosa Parks helpd start the civil rights movement inn 1955.

_____

_____

17. Identifyed as the most popular cowboy and cowgirl in history, this is what Roy Rogers and Dale Evans becomed.

_____

_____

18. Besides staring in cowboy movies Roy founded The Happy Trails Childrens Foundation with there wife, Dale.

_____

_____

19. Harry s Truman, an american president, declard, "the Bill of Rights applys to everybody, and dont you ever forgit it.

_____

_____

20. Milton hershey once said, i often hear people said that childran are not what them used to be. But i has the conviction that them is just what them always has been. Perhaps it be the parent's who has change.

_____

_____

_____

_____

3 Paragraph Composition

Just as words form sentences, so sentences form paragraphs. In Part One, we learned that good sentences are concise, clear, unified, varied, and interesting. A good paragraph has all these qualities too. Yet with paragraphs, we are thinking in "bigger" terms—how sentences relate to one another rather than how words do. Paragraphs themselves are the building blocks for essays, term papers, book reports, business letters, and so on. Mastering the techniques of effective paragraph composition, then, will go a long way toward ensuring your success in the critical skill of writing longer pieces.

The following lessons show you ways to create strong, unified paragraphs that hook your readers' interest and keep them reading.

9 The Paragraph

 A *paragraph* is a group of sentences telling about one topic.

For example, read the following two paragraphs about the subject of advertising.

No matter what you do or where you go, businesses confront you with commercials. Are you watching television? Expect plenty of "special messages from our sponsors." Are you listening to the radio? Be prepared for your favorite songs to be "coming right up after these words from local businesses." As you drive along the streets of town, billboards and business signs compete for your attention. The bus in front of you may display an advertisement on its back or sides. Is there any way to escape the bombardment of advertising?

Many people hoped that the Word Wide Web would be a fun place to cruise around, reading and chatting, without worrying about advertisements cropping up every two seconds. But as any Internet surfer knows, ad banners have become a fact of life. They pop up nearly wherever you go on the Net, whether to a merchant site, a news site, or even a page of search results. Not only that, but businesses inundate your e-mail account with unsolicited sales pitches, otherwise known as spam. Advertising, it seems, is here to stay, whether in traditional venues like billboards or in the newer venues of technology.

QUESTION: All the sentences are about the subject of advertising. Why, then, are the sentences split into two paragraphs?

ANSWER: It is true that all the sentences are about the same *general subject*. However, each paragraph has its own *specific topic*—its own point to make about the subject.

The first paragraph above tells about how people are confronted with advertisements. All sentences in this paragraph deal with this topic.

The second paragraph tells about advertisements on the Web. All sentences in this paragraph deal with this topic.

Note that the beginning of a paragraph is *indented;* that is, the first word is moved a short space to the right of the margin. Also note that an extra line of space is *not* included between paragraphs, whether in typed or handwritten compositions.

SUMMARY: A *paragraph* is a group of sentences telling about one topic. When you come to a new topic, begin a new paragraph. Remember to indent when you start a new paragraph.

Writing Paragraphs

Do you think businesses should be allowed to place posters or banners in school hallways to advertise their products to students and teachers? Brainstorm several reasons why this may be a good idea and several reasons why it may not be a good idea. Then choose the stronger set of reasons to use in writing your response.

On a separate sheet of paper, write **two** paragraphs in response to the above question. In the first paragraph, tell whether you do or do not think businesses should be allowed to advertise in school hallways and explain one reason why you think so. In the second paragraph, explain another reason to support your opinion.

Paragraph Length

QUESTION: How long should a paragraph be?

ANSWER: Quite simply, it should be as long as it needs to be.

A paragraph that is developing a topic does not consist of a predetermined number of sentences. However, very long paragraphs—say, a page long—can seem forbidding to readers. Often, paragraphs become very long due to a lack of organized thinking on the writer's part. Readers must think very hard to determine the main idea and how the supporting sentences connect to it. To avoid this problem, do the thinking for your readers by organizing paragraphs around one main idea, sticking to that idea, and starting a new paragraph for the next main idea.

Very short paragraphs—say, one or two sentences—may be used, but only with care. Sometimes the one-sentence paragraph can make a point dramatically. A series of one-sentence paragraphs, though, makes your writing disjointed and leaves the reader with the impression that you have not developed your subject. Again, do the thinking for your reader by developing one main idea per paragraph and making that idea very clear.

ACTIVITY

Write a two-paragraph passage beginning with the sentence *Many advertisements promise more than the product can realistically deliver.*

It is a good idea to write about advertisements you have actually seen. Here are examples of products commonly advertised:

snack foods (potato chips, sodas, etc.)   vehicles (cars, trucks)

weight-loss products   apparel (clothing, shoes)

cosmetics   fast food

Suggestions for the First Paragraph

1. Topic of first paragraph: *a misleading advertisement*

2. Give an example of an advertisement of one particular product and what the ad seems to promise viewers/readers/listeners.

Suggestions for the Second Paragraph

1. Topic of second paragraph: *a reality check.*

2. Explain why the advertised product does not deliver on the promise.

Before you start writing, look at the following sample passage, which shows one way of writing the two paragraphs.

Sample:

Many advertisements promise more than the product can realistically deliver. For example, some ads make viewers think that eating a certain brand of potato chips is an exciting and happy experience. In the ads, people sing and dance and toss chips into one another's mouths. Everyone seems incredibly carefree, attractive, and healthy, as though these potato chips have made every dream come true. The message: eat these chips and your life will be complete!

Well, I am here to tell you that eating potato chips—of any brand—does not solve life's problems. In fact, it can create problems. For example, eating potato chips can make you gain weight because they are high in fat. Eating chips can also put your health at risk in other ways because chips are not a healthful food. If you eat them instead of a healthful snack, you deprive your body of needed nutrients. Finally, if you eat chips in hopes of chasing away unhappiness, you will be disappointed. Potato chips do not solve emotional problems.

Now, on a separate sheet of paper, write your own two-paragraph passage.

Unity in the Paragraph

The key to effective paragraph writing is *unity*.

QUESTION: What is unity?

ANSWER: Unity comes from the Latin word *unus,* meaning "one." **Unity means "oneness."**

A paragraph has *unity* if it deals with *one* main topic and all its sentences stick to that topic—and contribute something to it.

Think back to the first two paragraphs in Lesson 9, about advertisements being everywhere. Suppose the first paragraph had been written this way:

1No matter what you do or where you go, businesses confront you with commercials. **2**This can become annoying, especially since advertisements are usually boring. **3**Ads for air fresheners are especially dull. **4**Who cares about that? **5**In addition, they interrupt your favorite television show or magazine article. **6**Sure, when you watch TV and hear, "And now a message from our sponsor," you can go grab a snack from the kitchen. **7**But wouldn't you rather see the whole show without commercials? **8**Shows with fewer commercials would be nice too. **9**Radio commercials are much the same. **10**Be prepared for your favorite songs to be "coming right up after these words from local businesses." **11**As you drive around town, being behind a bus belching diesel fumes is bad enough. **12**Having to read advertisements on its back is unpleasant, too. **13**Even if you try not to notice them, they still make an impression. **14**After all, you have to face forward with your eyes open if you want to drive safely.

QUESTION: Does the above paragraph have unity?

ANSWER: No. The sentences ramble about several main ideas and are not focused on one clear main idea.

The first sentence, S1, states what should be the main idea: *No matter what you do or where you go, businesses confront you with commercials.*

S2–S4 veer off topic by telling about the boring nature of advertisements.

S5 gets back on topic by giving an example of how businesses confront people with commercials.

S6–S8 veer off topic by focusing on snacks and a wish for fewer commercials.

S9–S10 get back on topic by giving an example of how businesses confront people with commercials.

S11 veers off topic by focusing on diesel fumes.

S12 gets back on topic by giving the example of advertisements on buses.

S12–S13 ramble, adding little (S12) or nothing (S13) to the paragraph's main idea.

In much of our writing, especially in first drafts, paragraphs will have a lack of unity. The problem often arises when a writer "follows a rabbit trail"—that is, lets one idea lead to the next until the main idea has been left far behind. The off-topic sentences rob the paragraph of unity, not to mention making it bulky and confusing.

ACTIVITY 1

Some of the following paragraphs have unity; some do not. Read each paragraph carefully and tell which sentences, if any, are off the topic.

Sample a

¹Propaganda is a form of advertising. ²It sells ideas, opinions, and points of view as fact. ³To accomplish its purpose, it uses catchy songs, zingy slogans, funny cartoons, juicy rumors, and more. ⁴Simply put, propaganda tries to convince people to believe or support a certain idea.

SENTENCES OFF TOPIC, IF ANY: _____ None _____

Sample b

¹Big businesses sometimes dump harmful waste. ²Some people fail to recycle simply because they lack a leader to motivate and guide them. ³You can be this leader in your family, your school, and your community. ⁴Start simple. ⁵For example, collect aluminum cans at your school for recycling, first checking with administration regarding applicable rules. ⁶Some companies make paper, boxes, and other products using recycled materials. ⁷After the program is organized, expand it to include paper and plastic.

SENTENCES OFF TOPIC, IF ANY: _____ Sentences 1 and 6 _____

Paragraph 1

¹Young adults under age eighteen are not old enough to vote; however, elected officials determine many aspects of these people's lives. ²One such aspect is young people's rights. ³At what age do they have the right to drive? ⁴At what age do they gain the right to vote? ⁵At what age can they legally get a job? ⁶What is the legal age for purchasing alcohol and cigarettes? ⁶Drinking and smoking can cause serious health problems. ⁷Teens under eighteen cannot vote on these issues, but they are very much affected by them.

SENTENCES OFF TOPIC, IF ANY: _____

Paragraph 2

¹The literal meaning of the word *democracy* is "rule by the people." ²We get the word from the Greek word *demokratia,* coined in the mid-fifth century B.C. ³It is formed of two

Greek words: *demos,* meaning "people," and *kratos,* meaning "rule." [4]The Greeks gave us many other words, too, such as *character, delta,* and *ecology.* [5]As this centuries-old word suggests, in a democratic political system, the people—not a king, queen, or dictator—rule. [6]About ten percent of English words have Greek origins.

SENTENCES OFF TOPIC, IF ANY: _____

Paragraph 3

[1]A person too young to vote should ignore politics until he or she turns eighteen, right? [2]Wrong! [3]A multitude of opportunities exist for young people to take political action and make their voices heard. [4]Teens and kids can hand out campaign literature in their neighborhoods. [5]They can post campaign signs and decorate cars and floats for parades. [6]At campaign headquarters, they can answer phones, type letters, and organize other volunteers (including adults). [7]Young people do have political power.

SENTENCES OFF TOPIC, IF ANY: _____

Paragraph 4

[1]In the United States, the two dominant political parties are the Democratic Party and the Republican Party, but other parties exist. [2]Another definition of *party* is "a fun social gathering." [3]A few examples are the Green Party, the Independence Party, the Communist Party USA, and the Reform Party, to name a few. [4]Over the years, these "third parties" grow or decline in power. [5]New ones form, and others fizzle out. [6]Some are more widely known than others, but all have specific political agendas (goals). [7]What is your political agenda? [8]Many have Web sites where citizens can learn more about them.

SENTENCES OFF TOPIC, IF ANY: _____

Paragraph 5

[1]A person convicted of a felony loses certain rights—sometimes permanently. [2]In many states, the felon is disenfranchised; that is, he or she loses the right to vote. [3]In ten states, one felony conviction is enough to receive permanent disenfranchisement. [4]Moreover, a felony conviction can prevent someone from obtaining certain jobs, such as teaching, and from being eligible for certain opportunities, such as receiving college financial aid. [5]Consequently, the punishment for a felony crime goes beyond the prison or probation sentence. [6]It affects the rest of the person's life.

SENTENCES OFF TOPIC, IF ANY: _____

QUESTION: Besides staying on topic, how else can I give my paragraphs unity?

ANSWER: Another aspect of unity among sentences is fitting together as a whole. That is, all sentences in a paragraph should relate to one another in a clear, logical way.

Read the following paragraph.

For someone who organizes a recycling program, multiple benefits exist. There is an environmental benefit. You enable the materials to be used again. They are not dumped. Organizing the program develops your leadership abilities. You get valuable practice making a plan and carrying it out. You probably overcame obstacles. You can use your accomplishment to your advantage. You can list the activity on applications for college, scholarships, and jobs. Your leadership and organizational skills are showcased.

Is this a strong, unified paragraph? No. It really could be much better. All of the sentences talk about the benefits of organizing a recycling program, but the sentences themselves seem choppy and somewhat unrelated.

Now read the revised paragraph:

[1]For someone who organizes a recycling program, multiple benefits exist. [2]First is the environmental benefit. [3]You enable the materials to be used again, not dumped. [4]Second, organizing the program develops your leadership abilities. [5]You get valuable practice making a plan and carrying it out, including overcoming obstacles. [6]Third, you can use your accomplishment to your advantage. [7]For example, you can list the activity on applications for college, scholarships, and jobs. [8]As a result, your leadership and organizational skills are showcased.

This paragraph is much stronger because the sentences are connected to one another, creating unity. Here are three ways in which unity among these sentences is created.

1. The words *First, Second,* and *Third* organize ideas in the paragraph in a logical sequence. (sentences 2, 4, and 6)

2. Shorter sentences are joined to longer, related ones to show the relationship between those ideas. (sentences 2 and 5)

3. The expressions *For example* and *As a result* clarify the relationship between sentences. (sentences 7 and 8)

These changes in sentence structure and word choice promote unity in the paragraph.

The following table lists transitional words and phrases that will help you create unity among the sentences in a paragraph. In addition, you can use many of these words and phrases to provide transitions between paragraphs, thereby strengthening the unity of an entire composition.

Transitional Words and Phrases

TO DO THIS . . .	USE . . .
Give an example	for example, for instance, such as, one reason, specifically, in particular, namely, to illustrate
Add information	and, also, in addition, another, besides, too, as well, moreover, next, what's more
Show effect, consequence, or conclusion	as a result, consequently, therefore, because of, for this reason, thus
Compare	similarly, likewise, both, at the same time, in the same way
Contrast	but, yet, in contrast, however, although, even though, while, otherwise, on the other hand, on the contrary, nevertheless, instead
Emphasize	most important, in particular, primarily, in fact, especially, above all, even more, obviously
Show sequence or time	first, second, third, next, after, before, soon, immediately, while, during, later, then, meanwhile, after a while, at last, last, finally, ultimately, in the past, in the future, since then, at the same time
Show place or direction	over, under, beside, around, nearby, close, far, in the distance, farther, closer, in front of, inside, outside, above, below, to the left, to the right
Summarize or bring to a close	in summary, to sum up, finally, lastly, in conclusion, for these reasons, to conclude, on the whole, in other words, in general, after all

 Writing Application

Using Transitions to Write a Unified Paragraph

Following the steps in a process is essential to achieving many different kinds of goals. Examples of such goals include

    election to an office (i.e., class president)

    completion of a project (i.e., teaching a puppy to sit or fetch)

    acquiring a skill (i.e., learning to use an e-mail software application)

    arriving at a destination (i.e., traveling from your house to a friend's)

    Choose one of the goals above, or think of a different goal that you know how to achieve. On a separate sheet of paper, write a paragraph telling readers how to achieve the goal. (Include approximately six to eight sentences.) In the topic sentence, be sure to identify the goal. Within the paragraph, use transitions to link ideas logically and smoothly.

Writing a Unified Paragraph

Do you think it is everyone's civic duty to vote whether he or she feels like it or not? Or do you think voting is a good—but optional—civic right? To develop your opinion, brainstorm several reasons why voting should be considered a civic duty and several reasons why it should be considered optional.

For which point of view did you list the strongest reasons? Use these reasons to write a paragraph that persuades readers to agree with your point of view. Make sure the paragraph has unity, adding or removing sentences and transitions as necessary.

LESSON The Topic Sentence

A strong paragraph usually has a topic sentence.

 A *topic sentence* states the topic, or main idea, of a paragraph.

Here are some of the topic sentences you have read in Lessons 9 and 10:

No matter what you do or where you go, businesses confront you with commercials. *(page 102)*

Many advertisements promise more than the product can realistically deliver. *(page 104)*

Propaganda is a form of advertising. *(page 106)*

Young adults under age eighteen are not old enough to vote; however, elected officials determine many aspects of these people's lives. *(page 106)*

A multitude of opportunities exist for young people to take political action and make their voices heard. *(page 107)*

For someone who organizes a recycling program, multiple benefits exist. *(page 108)*

QUESTION: Why are topic sentences useful?

ANSWER: Topic sentences help us read and write better.

When we read, the topic sentence tells us what the paragraph will be about. When we write a paragraph, if we keep referring back to our topic sentence, it will keep us from going off the topic.

Not all paragraphs begin with a topic sentence. Instead they build up to the main idea and then, lastly, state that idea. Other paragraphs imply the main idea without stating it directly in a topic sentence. In this lesson, however, we practice writing topic sentences that are stated directly and that come early in the paragraph because it is a good way to develop strong, basic skills in composition.

ACTIVITY 1

Write a paragraph beginning with one of the topic sentences listed below. Before you start writing, read the Sample Paragraph that follows the list of topic sentences.

Suggested Topic Sentences

   1. My school offers several opportunities for student leadership.

   2. The _____ team has had a good (*or* disappointing) season.

   4. If you don't have a car, there are other ways to get around town.

   3. Modern technology provides various ways to get in touch with friends.

   5. Pets sometimes surprise us with their cleverness.

   Your paragraph should consist of at least six or seven sentences. Here is a Sample Paragraph to use as a model.

Sample Paragraph:

¹My school offers several opportunities for student leadership. ²For those interested in sports such as soccer or cheerleading, serving as a team captain is rewarding. ³Being president of a club allows other students to flex their leadership muscles. ⁴Still others run for student council or class officer, or they sign up to be an after-school tutor. ⁵These are just a few of the many opportunities at Westwood. ⁶Any student who wants to lead can find a leadership role in his or her area of interest.

Comments: The sample paragraph consists of six sentences. The topic sentence (S1) states that *My school offers several opportunities for student leadership.* All the other sentences support this statement.

S2 gives an example of leadership in sports.

S3 gives an example of leadership in clubs.

S4 gives examples of leadership in the student body.

S5 points out that even more leadership opportunities exist.

S6 clinches the paragraph by stating that leadership roles exist for all who are interested.

Note that the paragraph has unity because it deals with one topic, and every sentence in the paragraph stays on the topic.

Now, write your paragraph on a separate sheet of paper.

QUESTION: How do I write a topic sentence?

ANSWER: A topic sentence says something specific about a topic. Before you write your sentence, answer these two questions, if only in your mind:

1. What is the topic of this paragraph?

2. What point am I making about this topic?

Once you've answered these questions, write a sentence that (1) identifies or makes clear the topic and (2) says something specific about that topic.

A topic sentence does not exist in isolation; rather, it is always part of a paragraph. The examples below show you how to write topic sentences for three sample school assignments that ask for complete paragraphs.

SCENARIO 1: You must write a paragraph about Martin Luther King, Jr. for history class. To write the topic sentence, you follow these steps:

STEP 1: What is the topic of this paragraph? *Martin Luther King, Jr.*

STEP 2: What point am I making about Martin Luther King, Jr.? *He was awarded the Nobel Peace Prize in 1964. It was to honor his civil rights work.*

TOPIC SENTENCE: *Martin Luther King, Jr. earned the Nobel Peace Prize in 1964 for his efforts to advance civil rights.*

COMMENTS: The body of this paragraph should give examples of King's actions that earned him the award.

SCENARIO 2:   You must answer the following test question with a complete paragraph: What is the basic structure of the United Sates government? To write the topic sentence, you follow these steps:

STEP 1:   What is the topic of this paragraph? *the structure of the U.S. government.*

STEP 2:   What point am I making about the structure of the U.S. government? *I am identifying the structure, which has three parts: the legislative branch, the executive branch, and the judicial branch.*

TOPIC SENTENCE: *The structure of the U.S. government includes three main branches: the legislative, the executive, and the judicial.*

COMMENTS: The body of this paragraph should explain the basic purpose of each of the three branches.

SCENARIO 3:   You must answer this question using a complete paragraph: What is the main conflict in *Romeo and Juliet*? To write the topic sentence, you follow these steps:

STEP 1:   What is the topic of this paragraph? *conflict in <u>Romeo and Juliet</u>*

STEP 2:   What point am I making about the conflict in this play? *I am identifying the main conflict, which is the feud between the Capulets and the Montagues.*

TOPIC SENTENCE: *The main conflict in <u>Romeo and Juliet</u> is the feud between the Capulets and the Montagues.*

COMMENTS: The body of this paragraph should prove that this is, indeed, the *main* conflict by telling how other conflicts are caused by it or grow out of it.

ACTIVITY 2

Write topic sentences that follow the instructions below.

> **Samples:**
>
> **a.** Write a topic sentence for a paragraph about e-mail.
>
> E-mail is quick and convenient, but it can never take the place of a thoughtful handwritten note.
>
> **b.** Write a topic sentence for a paragraph about airport security.
>
> The "power tool" of airport security is the baggage X-ray machine.

1. Write a topic sentence for a paragraph about the cost of movie tickets.

_____

_____

2. Write a topic sentence for a paragraph about a school rule.

_____

_____

3. Write a topic sentence for a paragraph about rap music.

_____

_____

4. Write a topic sentence for a paragraph about cheating on exams.

_____

_____

5. Write a topic sentence for a paragraph about first dates.

_____

_____

Writing Application   Using a Topic Sentence in a Paragraph

Choose one of the topic sentences you wrote in Activity 3 and use it to write a complete paragraph. Make sure that each sentence in the paragraph stays on topic and helps explain or prove the topic sentence. Write your paragraph on a separate sheet of paper.

Writing Application   Writing a Paragraph with a Strong Topic Sentence

Choose one of the following topics and write a complete paragraph about it. To develop the paragraph, you may want to explain an opinion about the topic, prove a point about the topic, or tell facts about the topic.

In your paragraph, include a topic sentence that states something specific about the topic and body sentences that explain or prove the topic sentence. Write your paragraph on a separate sheet of paper.

Suggested Topics

women's football	shoplifting	privacy at home
Abraham Lincoln	gossip	white lies
software piracy	guitar music	fame

12 The Clincher Sentence

A clincher sentence can strengthen your paragraph by emphasizing the main idea.

 A *clincher sentence* drives home the point that the paragraph is making.

Not all paragraphs have a clincher sentence. When there is one, it is usually the last sentence in the paragraph.

A good clincher sentence restates the main idea already mentioned in the topic sentence, but it does so more strongly, with the help of material brought out in the paragraph. A clincher sentence should not merely repeat the topic sentence.

Recall the following paragraph from Lesson 11.

1My school offers several opportunities for student leadership. **2**For those interested in sports such as soccer or cheerleading, serving as a team captain is rewarding. **3**Being president of a club allows other students to flex their leadership muscles. **4**Still others run for student council or class officer, or they sign up to be an after-school tutor. **5**These are just a few of the many opportunities at Westwood. **6**Any student who wants to lead can find a leadership role in his or her area of interest.

In this paragraph, the clincher sentence, S6, drives home the point that numerous leadership opportunities exist at the school. However, S6 does not merely restate the topic sentence, S1. It builds on details in the paragraph, which tell about specific leadership roles. To clinch the paragraph, S6 uses key words and ideas from the entire paragraph—the topic sentence and the body sentences. In S6, these key words are *student, leadership,* and *interest*.

The following paragraph is complete except for the clincher sentence. What would be a good clincher sentence to end this paragraph?

One of the delights of poetry is its use of sound. For instance, onomatopoeia is the use of words that sound like the sound they represent. *Moo, clip-clop,* and *chug* are examples. Another appealing use of sound is alliteration. Using this literary device, the poet selects a series of words starting with the same sound. Who wouldn't enjoy reading about a *slippery, slinky, slimy snake?* Of course, the most common use of sound is the rhyme. Many, though not all, poems have a regular pattern of lines ending with the same sound.

QUESTIONS: Of the following sentences, which two would be strong clincher sentences for the above paragraph? Why? Which would be weak clincher sentences, and why?

CHOICE 1. A couplet is a set of two lines that rhyme, and a quatrain is a set of four lines with a rhyming pattern.

CHOICE 2. Onomatopoeia, alliteration, and rhyme are just a few of the delightful uses of sound in poetry.

CHOICE 3. In these ways and more, poetry charms the ear with sound imitation, sound repetition, and rhyme.

CHOICE 4. Overall, sound is one of the pleasures of poetry.

ANSWERS: Choices 2 and 3 each would make a strong clincher sentence. Choice 2 sums up the key words in the body of the paragraph and ties them to main idea in the topic sentence. Choice 3 restates the main ideas a little differently from choice 2 and, in addition, alludes to a bigger picture with the words "and more." Both choices drive home the point of the topic sentence while expanding on it using details from the paragraph.

Choices 1 and 4 each would make a weak clincher sentence. Choice 1 gives more details about the third point in the paragraph, rhyme. It does not, however, tie together the ideas in the whole paragraph. Choice 4 merely rephrases the topic sentence.

ACTIVITY 1

Decide which sentence (A, B, or C) would make the best clincher sentence for the following paragraph. Write the letter of your choice on the blank and then explain why it is a good clincher sentence.

Haiku and tanka depend upon the syllable for their poetic structures. Haiku consists of three unrhymed lines. Specifically, line 1 has five syllables, line 2 has seven syllables, and line 3 has five syllables, for a total of seventeen syllables. Tanka is a five-line poem, also unrhymed. Each of the lines has a syllable count of five, seven, five, seven, and seven, in that order.

Choices:

A. An amazing array of beautiful haikus and tankas can come from these simple, syllable-based structures.

B. Both of these are forms of Japanese poetry.

C. Syllables are the building blocks for both haiku and tanka, which are forms of Japanese poetry.

CLINCHER SENTENCE: _____

WHY IT IS GOOD: _____

_____

_____

ACTIVITY 2

Decide which sentence (A, B, or C) would make the best clincher sentence for the following paragraph. Write the letter of your choice on the blank and then explain why it is a good clincher sentence.

Poetry is all about beauty and sentimentality, right? Not necessarily. One fun, irreverent form of poetry is the grue. Short for *gruesome,* the grue celebrates ghastly subject matter in a witty manner. Writers of grues spin rhymes about unlucky accidents, unfortunate endings, and unlawful actions. Dreadful acts and accidents abound in these poems, but always with a comic twist.

Choices:

A. In summary, the grue is fun and irreverent.

B. Some people may be offended by the horrors in grues, and these readers should simply set aside the poetry.

C. Not to be taken literally, these gruesome rhymes are simply a cheeky form of entertainment.

CLINCHER SENTENCE: _____

WHY IT IS GOOD: _____

_____

_____

ACTIVITY 3 _____

Write a suitable clincher sentence for the following paragraph. Then explain why it is a good one.

Figures of speech such as metaphors and similes allow poets to express ideas in appealing ways. The metaphor compares two unlike things, suggesting qualities of one thing in another. For example, a poet may write *Rodney's ego was the size of a bus.* Comparing the ego to a bus is more interesting than saying *Rodney had a big ego.* Similes, too, make comparisons, except they use the word *like, as,* or *than.* To express the same idea using a simile, the poet could write *Rodney's ego was bigger than a bus.*

CLINCHER SENTENCE: _____

_____

_____

WHY IT IS GOOD: _____

_____

_____

ACTIVITY 4 _____

Write a suitable clincher sentence for the following paragraph. Then explain why it is a good one.

Musical artists who write their own lyrics are not just singers; they are poets. First of all, a person who writes a song uses the same skills as a poet. For example, he or she expresses ideas in lines set in stanzas, like stanzas in a poem. Besides that, songwriters often use rhyming lines, and rhyme is a key tool of the poet. In addition, a songwriter must call upon literary creativity, just like a poet. In particular, he or she must express ideas in creative, lyrical, imaginative ways instead of in flat sentences.

CLINCHER SENTENCE: _____

_____

_____

WHY IT IS GOOD: _____

_____

_____

ACTIVITY 5 _____

Write a suitable clincher sentence for the following paragraph. Then explain why it is a good one.

A concrete poem's theme relates to its shape. For example, a concrete poem about a Christmas tree might have a short first line, centered. Then the second line would be a little longer, also centered. Each successive line would be longer, until they all formed a triangle—suggesting the tree. At the bottom, several shorter lines would form the trunk. The entire poem expresses the idea of a Christmas tree. Other popular shapes or topics for concrete poems are a kite, a snake, a heart, and a raindrop.

CLINCHER SENTENCE: _____

_____

_____

WHY IT IS GOOD: _____

_____

_____

 Writing
Application

Writing a Paragraph With a Clincher Sentence

Do you like reading poetry? Why or why not? To develop your answer, brainstorm a list of reasons why you do or don't enjoy reading poems. Choose the strongest reasons to use in writing your response.

Using the ideas developed in your prewriting, write a paragraph of at least **six** sentences, answering the questions above. Make sure the paragraph has a clincher sentence that drives home the point of the topic sentence.

Developing a Paragraph With Examples

Thus far in Part Three, the lessons have emphasized how paragraphs must have unity. Achieving that unity, however, is not always easy. Fortunately, there are some practical methods that can help. First, though, you must know the *purpose* of your paragraph.

Paragraphs serve many different purposes. In school, most of the paragraphs you write will *inform* your reader of information or *persuade* readers to accept your point of view on a topic. In this lesson, we examine how to develop unified informative paragraphs. In Lesson 14, we will examine how to develop unified persuasive paragraphs.

An *informative paragraph* tells readers essential information about one main idea.

Recall this informative paragraph from Lesson 12.

[1]One of the delights of poetry is its use of sound. [2]For instance, onomatopoeia is the use of words that sound like the sound they represent. [3]*Moo, clip-clop,* and *chug* are examples. [4]Another appealing use of sound is alliteration. [5]Using this literary device, the poet selects a series of words starting with the same sound. [6]Who wouldn't enjoy reading about a *slippery, slinky, slimy snake?* [7]Of course, the most common use of sound is the rhyme. [8]Many, though not all, poems have a regular pattern of lines ending with the same sound. [9]In these ways and more, poetry charms the ear with sound imitation, sound repetition, and rhyme.

This informative paragraph is developed using *examples.* Examples not only add interest to a paragraph, they also explain and clarify the main idea by offering valuable details. As a result, readers are able to fully understand the idea expressed in the topic sentence.

Look more closely at the paragraph. S1 (the topic sentence) states that *One of the delights of poetry is its use of sound.* The supporting sentences in the paragraph explain the use of sound by means of *examples:*

EXAMPLE 1: onomatopoeia (S2–S3)

EXAMPLE 2: alliteration (S4–S6)

EXAMPLE 3: rhyme (S7–S8)

Finally, S9 clinches the paragraph.

Each topic sentence below can be developed into a paragraph by using *examples*. Two examples are listed. Add a third.

> **Samples:**
>
> **a.** TOPIC SENTENCE: Friends meet specific needs in our lives.
>
> EXAMPLES:　　**1.** They provide companionship.
>
> 　　　　　　　**2.** They help us through hard times.
>
> 　　　　　　　**3.** They push us to be our personal best.
>
> **b.** TOPIC SENTENCE: Dolphins and humans have traits in common.
>
> EXAMPLES:　　**1.** We are both mammals.
>
> 　　　　　　　**2.** We live in families.
>
> 　　　　　　　**3.** We communicate using a language.

1. TOPIC SENTENCE: Water lovers enjoy certain vacation destinations.

EXAMPLES:　　**1.** lakes

　　　　　　　2. water parks

　　　　　　　3. _____

2. TOPIC SENTENCE: Each of us can do something to conserve energy.

EXAMPLES:　　**1.** We can ride a bicycle to school.

　　　　　　　2. We can turn off the television when we leave the room.

　　　　　　　3. _____

3. TOPIC SENTENCE: Making macaroni and cheese involves three basic steps.

EXAMPLES:　　**1.** Boil then drain the macaroni.

　　　　　　　2. Grate the cheese.

　　　　　　　3. _____

4. TOPIC SENTENCE: The Wildcats won the game in the final three seconds.

EXAMPLES:　　**1.** Kareem passed the ball to Nigel.

　　　　　　　2. Nigel went in for a layup shot.

　　　　　　　3. _____

5. TOPIC SENTENCE: Commas serve several purposes in sentences.

    EXAMPLES: **1.** They set off an introductory phrase or clause.

               2. They set off an appositive.

               3. _____

Look back at the items in Activity 1. Each is a basic outline for a paragraph (topic sentence plus supporting examples). To write a well-developed paragraph using such an outline, *be sure to develop each example fully.* Do not simply list several examples and then end the paragraph. For example, suppose the paragraph about sound in poetry had been written like this:

One of the delights of poetry is its use of sound. For instance, onomatopoeia is one creative use of sound. Another appealing use of sound is alliteration. Also, many poems have a regular pattern of rhyming lines. In these ways and more, poetry charms the ear with sound imitation, sound repetition, and rhyme.

This paragraph has a topic sentence and supporting examples, but the examples are not developed fully. The reader learns that onomatopoeia, alliteration, and rhyme are examples of the use of sound, but they are left wondering what exactly each of these techniques is. The paragraph is much stronger when it contains detailed explanations of each example, as shown on page 119.

 Writing
Application

Writing an Informative Paragraph

Using one of the paragraph ideas in Activity 1, write a complete paragraph (use at least **six** sentences). Support and explain the topic with at least **three** fully developed examples. You can use examples listed in the activity or come up with others. If you wish, add a clincher sentence to conclude the paragraph. Write your paragraph on a separate sheet of paper.

Arranging the Examples

When you write a paragraph containing several examples, consider the *organizational pattern* of the paragraph. Do not simply leave the examples in the order in which they occurred to you. Instead, put some thought into organizing the examples effectively.

QUESTION: If I include strong examples in my paragraph, shouldn't that be good enough? Why should I care how the examples are arranged?

ANSWER: The order of your examples affects the reader's response to your writing. The reader's response includes his or her level of interest in your paragraph, understanding of your points, and acceptance of what you've written. An effective organizational pattern helps your reader get the most out of your paragraph.

You want to grab your reader's interest right away with a strong example. You want to end on an even stronger note. Therefore, begin with a strong example, but not your strongest. End the paragraph with your strongest example (or put it just before the clincher sentence if there is one).

Study the order of the examples in the following paragraph.

¹This summer, students from Collin County Community College gave the school's grassy quad* a much-needed update. ²Since hundreds of tramping feet had worn dirt trails through the grass, students brought in gravel to cover the paths. ³They set weatherproof benches beside the walks, along with new trash and recycling receptacles. ⁴In one corner, they erected a community bulletin board. ⁵Most important, they installed an emergency call box at each corner of the quad. ⁶These improvements, funded completely by alumni donations, have made the grassy quad a safe and popular student gathering place.

*quad: quadrangle; a four-sided area enclosed by buildings

This paragraph informs readers of the facts of a campus improvement project. The topic sentence (S1) states that students *gave the school's "grassy quad" a much-needed update.* The supporting sentences provide detailed examples of the improvements, building up to the most important example.

The first example (in S2) is strong enough to get readers' interest. The facts about the grass, worn paths, and gravel pertain to a big, noticeable change. Smaller, though significant, changes come next (in S3–S4), completing the mental picture of the entire area. The final example (in S5), which emphasizes an improvement to student safety, is the strongest; it provides a powerful finish to the series of examples. Finally, S6 clinches the paragraph.

ACTIVITY 2

Choose one of the following topic sentences and develop it into a paragraph by giving examples. You may use a topic sentence of your own, if you wish. Before you begin writing, read the sample paragraph and comments that follow.

Suggested Topic Sentences

1. My family's pet _____ (dog, etc.) is a valuable member of the household.
2. Preparing for a job interview involves a few essential steps.
3. Allergies afflict many people, young and old.
4. An action-adventure film has certain basic qualities.
5. There are several stages to preparing for a test.

> **Sample:**
>
> ¹There are several stages to preparing for a test. ²Preparation begins long before the night before the test. ³To do your best, you must attend all classes, pay attention, and take notes. ⁴Ask questions whenever a concept is unclear. ⁵With this foundation, the rest of your preparation has the best chance of success. ⁶A few days before the test, study your notes, underlining key concepts. ⁷Again, ask your teacher questions if necessary. ⁸If you know that the test will be an essay test, practice writing paragraphs about the material, focusing on using strong topic sentences with relevant examples. ⁹Finally, don't forget to get a good night's sleep before the test. ¹⁰A rested brain allows all your previous preparation to pay off.

Comments: S1, the topic sentence, states *There are several stages to preparing for a test.*

S2–S10 (the rest of the paragraph) support the statement with *examples.*

S3 and S4 give the first few examples: attend class, pay attention, take notes, ask questions.

S5 emphasizes the importance of these examples while providing a transition to the rest of the examples.

S6–S8 give more examples: study, ask questions, practice writing paragraphs.

S9 and S10 give the final example: get a good night's sleep to get the most out of all previous preparation.

This paragraph does not have—or need—a clincher sentence. The last sentence (S10) is emphatic and gives closure.

Now, write your own paragraph on a separate sheet of paper. Edit the paragraph to make sure the examples build up to the strongest. Then, on the same page underneath the paragraph, explain why you arranged the examples in the order that you did.

QUESTION: How else can I organize examples in an informative paragraph?

ANSWER: Use an organizational method that works well with your subject matter. Various methods are described in the following table.

Methods of Arranging Examples

Increasing importance	Begin with the least important example and build up to the most important. This method causes your paragraph to gain strength sentence by sentence.
Chronological	When examples relate to a time sequence, give them in the order in which they happened. This method creates a logical, easy-to-follow presentation of ideas.
Sequence	When examples give steps in a process, give them in order from first to last. This method, too, creates a logical easy-to-follow presentation of ideas.
Compare and contrast	When comparing two things, group examples of like qualities together, and group examples of unlike qualities together.

Each topic sentence below can be developed into a paragraph with the examples listed. Number the examples to indicate the order in which they should be used. Then, on the lines provided, explain why you chose the order that you did.

Samples:

a. TOPIC SENTENCE: People often wrongly assume that my brother and I are identical twins.

EXAMPLES: ___1___ We have the same color and style of hair.

___3___ He is two inches taller than I am.

___2___ We have the same color eyes.

EXPLANATION: I grouped the similarities together as examples 1 and 2.
Since the difference between the brothers is most important in showing
that they are not identical, I gave that example last.

b. TOPIC SENTENCE: To write an essay, follow a reliable writing process.

EXAMPLES: ___3___ Write a rough draft.

___1___ Brainstorm ideas.

___2___ Prepare an outline.

___4___ Edit and polish the draft.

EXPLANATION: These examples explain a process, so I arranged them in the
order in which they should occur.

1. TOPIC SENTENCE: The last employee to leave the lab each night should perform specific tasks.

EXAMPLES: _____ Turn out the lights.

_____ Make sure all chemical vials are securely sealed.

_____ Lock the door from the outside.

_____ Make sure ALL hazardous waste has been disposed of in appropriate receptacles.

EXPLANATION: _____

_____

_____

2. TOPIC SENTENCE: An avalanche developed suddenly today on a ski slope.

EXAMPLES: _____ A section of snow broke loose and crashed down the slope.

_____ A loud shout apparently set off vibrations on the slope.

_____ Skiers safely used the slope for three hours.

EXPLANATION: _____

_____

_____

3. TOPIC SENTENCE: A DVD player is both similar to and different from a VCR.

EXAMPLES: _____ Both have fast forward and reverse options.

_____ Both have a play function.

_____ Only the VCR can record as well as play movies.

_____ Both have freeze frame capability.

EXPLANATION: _____

_____

_____

4. TOPIC SENTENCE: Living on your own carries responsibilities.

EXAMPLES: _____ Take your job seriously because you can't live on your own without that paycheck.

_____ Follow all rules of your apartment complex.

_____ Make a budget and stick to it.

_____ Pay your rent on time, or you'll find yourself living back with your parents.

EXPLANATION: _____

_____

_____

5. TOPIC SENTENCE: You can make a low-fat omelet.

EXAMPLES: _____ Store the yolks in the refrigerator to use in another dish.

_____ In a hot skillet, melt a pat of butter.

_____ Cook, flipping once, until whites are no longer runny.

_____ Add egg whites, chopped onions, salt, and pepper.

_____ Crack three eggs, carefully separating yolks from whites.

_____

_____

Writing Application

Arranging Examples in an Informative Paragraph

Choose one of the following topic sentences and develop it into a paragraph by giving examples. If you wish, use a topic sentence of your own. Make sure the examples in your paragraph are arranged in an order that best fits the subject matter. Write your paragraph on a separate sheet of paper.

Suggested Topic Sentences

1. Some drivers have horrible road manners.

2. Before you turn in a composition, edit it for errors.

3. Housecats and wildcats have similarities and differences.

14 Developing a Paragraph With Reasons

In this lesson, we examine how to develop persuasive paragraphs.

 A *persuasive paragraph* attempts to convince readers to agree with a particular point of view or to take a specific action.

Recall this persuasive paragraph from Lesson 12.

[1]Musical artists who write their own lyrics are not just singers; they are poets. [2]First of all, a person who writes a song uses the same skills as a poet. [3]For example, he or she expresses ideas in lines set in stanzas, like stanzas in a poem. [4]Besides that, songwriters often use rhyming lines, and rhyme is a key tool of the poet. [5]In addition, a songwriter must call upon literary creativity, just like a poet. [6]In particular, he or she must express ideas in creative, lyrical, imaginative ways instead of in flat sentences. [7]Clearly, songs are poems set to music, and an artist who writes a song writes a poem.

This persuasive paragraph is developed using *reasons,* or arguments.

Look more closely at the paragraph. S1 (the topic sentence) states that *Musical artists who write their own lyrics are not just singers; they are poets.* The supporting sentences persuade readers to accept this idea—that songwriters are poets—by offering *reasons:*

REASON 1: Songwriters and poets use the same skills (S2, S3).

REASON 2: Songwriters and poets use rhyme (S4).

REASON 3: Songwriters and poets use literary creativity (S5, S6).

Finally, S7 clinches the paragraph by driving home the paragraph's main idea.

ACTIVITY 1

Each topic sentence below can be developed into a paragraph by using *reasons*. Two reasons are listed. Add a third.

Samples:

a. TOPIC SENTENCE: Give country-western music a try.

REASONS: **1.** Many of the songs have a good dance beat.

2. The songs tell interesting stories about relationships.

3. The music is no longer the stereotypical "hillbilly" style of years past.

b. TOPIC SENTENCE: Parents should never look through their children's things without permission.

REASONS:

1. Everyone—including children and teenagers—has a right to privacy.

2. Snooping is cowardly; instead, parents should directly ask what they want to know.

3. _Snooping leads to arguments and lack of trust._

1. TOPIC SENTENCE: The school week should be four days long, with the fifth day reserved for doing homework.

REASONS:

1. Many students do not do their homework because they simply don't have time.

2. Students learn by listening, but they learn more by *doing*—doing homework, that is.

3. _____

2. TOPIC SENTENCE: The school library needs at least ten more computers for student use.

REASONS:

1. At least five students are always waiting for each computer.

2. Students are limited to twenty minutes on a computer, but this is insufficient time to complete an assignment.

3. _____

3. TOPIC SENTENCE: It is time for Coach DeMarco to retire.

REASONS:

1. His assistant coach does all the work.

2. He often misses the team's practices.

3. _____

4. TOPIC SENTENCE: Hugs and kisses in high school hallways should be banned.

REASONS:

1. Public displays of affection are annoying or disgusting to other people.

2. Couples who stop to hug and kiss are often late to the next class.

3. _____

5. TOPIC SENTENCE: Students who have an A average should not have to take the semester's final exam.

REASONS:

1. They have already proved that they know the material.

2. One more grade in their averages will not alter their final grades.

3. _____

QUESTION: Are several good reasons sufficient to make a successful persuasive paragraph?

ANSWER: Not necessarily. Strong reasons are essential, but you must fully develop each one. It is not enough simply to list reasons and expect readers to accept them. For example, suppose the paragraph about songwriters and poets had been written like this:

1Musical artists who write their own lyrics are not just singers; they are poets. **2**First of all, a person who writes a song uses the same skills as a poet. **3**Besides that, songwriters often use rhyming lines. **4**In addition, a songwriter must call upon literary creativity. **5**Clearly, songs are poems set to music, and an artist who writes a song writes a poem.

This paragraph offers three reasons why songwriters should be considered poets. Unfortunately, the reasons are vague or poorly developed.

- S2 claims that a songwriter uses the same skills as a poet, but no examples of such skills are offered.
- S3 is a little stronger, since most readers know that poems often use rhyming lines. However, readers must call upon this knowledge and then strive to make this comparison between poems and songs on their own. Few readers will take the time to do so.
- S4 is another vague statement that makes little sense without some sort of explanation.

Because of these undeveloped reasons, this paragraph is weak and unpersuasive.

As a writer, you must do the thinking for your readers, as mentioned in Lesson 9. How does that relate to persuasive writing? If you want to persuade readers of an idea, you should not only supply valid supporting reasons but also "connect the dots" for readers. That is, explain the reasons, give examples if necessary, and tell readers clearly how the reason proves the claim you made in the topic sentence. Doing these tasks produces strong, convincing paragraphs. Even if a reader does not completely agree with you, he or she may concede that you made some good points, nevertheless.

 Writing Application

Writing a Persuasive Paragraph

Using one of the paragraph ideas in Activity 1, write a persuasive paragraph (use at least **six** sentences). Be sure to fully develop each supporting reason. You can use reasons listed in the activity or come up with others. If you wish, add a clincher sentence to conclude the paragraph. Write your paragraph on a separate sheet of paper.

Arranging the Reasons

QUESTION: What is the best way to arrange reasons in a persuasive paragraph?

ANSWER: Reasons, like examples, should be arranged in an order that builds toward the strongest, or most convincing one. Keep in mind that *all* reasons should be relevant and convincing. But saving the best for last leaves readers with your most convincing reason uppermost in their minds.

Study the order of the reasons in the following paragraph, taken from Lesson 10.

1For someone who organizes a recycling program, multiple benefits exist. **2**First is the environmental benefit. **3**You enable the materials to be used again, not dumped. **4**Second, organizing the program develops your leadership abilities. **5**You get valuable practice making a plan and carrying it out, including overcoming obstacles. **6**Third, you can use your accomplishment to your advantage. **7**For example, you can list the activity on applications for college, scholarships, and jobs. **8**As a result, your leadership and organizational skills are showcased.

The goal of this paragraph is to persuade readers that *For someone who organizes a recycling program, multiple benefits exist* (S1). To persuade readers, the writer includes supporting reasons, each of which identifies and explains a benefit:

1. environmental benefit (materials are reused, not dumped)

2. personal accomplishment (development of leadership abilities)

3. personal advantage (showcase leadership and organization skills)

The writer offers a strong—though not the strongest—benefit first: the environmental benefit. Readers are likely to accept this reason and move on, wondering about other benefits. The reasons build toward the one that is most beneficial to the program organizer: the ability to list such an accomplishment on important applications.

ACTIVITY 2

Each topic sentence below can be developed into a paragraph with the reasons listed. Number the reasons to indicate the best order in which to use them.

> **Samples:**
>
> **a.** TOPIC SENTENCE: When it comes to friendship, opposites do not attract.
>
> REASONS: __3__ You have no interests in common, so you have nothing to do when you are together.
>
> __2__ You have no friends in common, so you end up alone together.
>
> __1__ You have no experiences in common, so you don't understand each other.
>
> *Comments:* Reason 1 is strong, pointing out why such a friendship would be difficult to begin. Reason 2 is stronger, pointing out social limits to such a friendship. Reason 3 is strongest, for even if you get past reasons 1 and 2, you can't overcome reason 3: having nothing to do when together.
>
> **b.** TOPIC SENTENCE: Your sandwich may be less healthful than you think.
>
> REASONS: __2__ Mayonnaise adds artery-clogging fat.
>
> __3__ Many cold cuts are packed with fillers (think "meat scraps") and artery-clogging fat.
>
> __1__ Pickles add a superdose of salt, which can contribute to water-retention (bloating).
>
> *Comments:* Reason 1 is best first since it names the least life-threatening detail. Reason 2 is stronger since it names a more serious problem. Reason 3 is strongest since it names both a disgusting detail (meat scraps) *and* a serious problem.

1. TOPIC SENTENCE: I have decided to quit the baseball team.

   REASONS: _____ My grades have fallen sharply due to neglected studies.

   _____ I do not need the exercise.

   _____ Practice times are inconvenient to me.

2. TOPIC SENTENCE: When it comes to friendship, opposites attract.

   REASONS: _____ You introduce each other to new activities.

   _____ You provide strength where the other person is weak.

   _____ You enlarge your social circles by sharing each other's friends.

3. TOPIC SENTENCE: Alcohol abuse is a serious problem.

   REASONS: _____ It can kill you, whether by a drunken accident or by liver disease.

   _____ It leads to dangerous behaviors.

   _____ It is an expensive habit and can drain your wallet dry.

4. TOPIC SENTENCE: You should purchase the optional warranty on expensive products.

   REASONS: _____ It is useful if the product breaks.

   _____ It provides peace of mind.

   _____ It is less expensive than the cost of the repairs it covers.

5. TOPIC SENTENCE: You should not purchase optional warranties on expensive products.

   REASONS: _____ Warranties do not cover all possible problems.

   _____ Most people never use a warranty they paid extra for.

   _____ Buying warranties for every product costs more than one or two repairs.

ACTIVITY 3

Using one of the following topic sentences, write your own paragraph developed with *reasons*. First, read the suggested topic sentences, the sample paragraph, and the comments. Then get started on your own paragraph by jotting down your reasons and arranging them in the most effective order. Finally, write your paragraph.

Suggested Topic Sentences

1. The most valuable things in life are free.

2. No one outgrows the joy of playing with toys.

3. A little white lie is (*or* is not) harmless.

4. Expensive sports cars are (*or* are not) worth the money.

5. Older siblings should (*or* should not) have to babysit younger siblings.

Sample Paragraph:

¹Older siblings should not have to babysit younger siblings. ²First of all, older kids have more homework and household chores than younger kids. ³Consequently, the older siblings do not have time to babysit. ⁴Second, younger kids often resent being watched by older siblings, and with good reason. ⁵Who wants to be bossed around by Big Sister or Big Brother? ⁶Forcing siblings into this situation only causes trouble. ⁷Finally, forcing older kids into the role of parents is unfair to both the older and younger siblings. ⁸As long as parents or guardians run the household, they should provide the parenting and let the kids—of whatever age—be kids.

Comments: S1 (the topic sentence) states that *Older siblings should not have to babysit younger siblings.* S2–S8 (the body of the paragraph) support the statement with *reasons.*

REASON 1: the lack of available time (S2–S3)

REASON 2: the unwillingness of the younger siblings (S4–S6)

REASON 3: the unfairness of such an arrangement (S7–S8)

The final sentence (S8) doubles as a clincher sentence. It not only emphasizes the idea (in S7) that siblings should not have to behave as parents but also reinforces the paragraph's main idea that siblings should not have to babysit siblings.

The reasons build from strong to stronger to strongest. Reason 1 mentions a simple problem of time. Reason 2 warns that sibling babysitting leads to trouble—a more pressing problem than time. Reason 3 attacks the wisdom of such an arrangement, and this reason would be powerful even if reasons 1 and 2 were not present.

Now, develop and write your own paragraph on a separate sheet of paper.

 Writing
Application

Arranging Reasons in a Persuasive Paragraph

Choose one of the following topic sentences and develop it into a paragraph by giving reasons. If you wish, use a topic sentence of your own. Make sure the reasons in your paragraph build toward the strongest reason. Write your paragraph on a separate sheet of paper.

Suggested Topic Sentences

1. Coed sports teams are (*or* are not) a good idea.

2. It is (*or* is not yet) time that we elected a woman to be the U.S. president.

3. Every child should (*or* should not have to) learn to play a musical instrument.

Introductory and Conclusion Paragraphs

A composition such as an essay or article is made up of three kinds of paragraphs:

1. introductory paragraph

2. body paragraph

3. conclusion paragraph

In Lessons 13 and 14, you reviewed methods of developing paragraphs with examples and reasons. Typically, these kinds of paragraphs form the body of a composition; they are *body paragraphs.* No composition is complete, however, without an *introduction* to these body paragraphs and a *conclusion* that summarizes and reinforces their key points.

Introductory Paragraphs

An *introductory paragraph* tells readers what to expect from the composition.

 The *introduction,* usually the first paragraph of a composition, introduces the paper's topic, states the paper's thesis (controlling idea), and identifies the paper's main points.

Read this example of an introductory paragraph:

Advertising is big business, helping companies to attract new customers and keep the ones they already have. In fact, the advertisement industry seems to know just where we, the consumers, are, and how to get their ads in front of our faces. Advertisements, also called commercials, are talented shape-shifters, appearing in print, on television, and on the Web. Consequently, encountering ads is a fact of life. Whether we like it or not, advertisements are inescapable and intrusive; some are actually misleading.

This introductory paragraph identifies the **topic** of the composition. To discover this topic, ask yourself what most of the sentences are about. They are about *advertisements*.

The paragraph also states the composition's **thesis**, or *controlling idea,* which states a specific viewpoint about the topic. Here, the thesis statement is the final sentence: *Whether we like it or not, advertisements are inescapable and intrusive; some are actually misleading.*

The thesis not only states a specific viewpoint about the topic but also identifies the **main points** to be developed in the composition. By examining S5, you can see that the main points are the ideas that advertisements are (1) *inescapable,* (2) *intrusive,* and (3) *misleading.*

QUESTION: Why are introductory paragraphs necessary?

ANSWER: Introductory paragraphs help us read and write compositions better. When we read, the introductory paragraph tells us what the composition will be about. When we write, if we keep referring back to our introductory paragraph, we will stay on topic and will be sure to include the relevant examples or reasons.

QUESTION: An introductory paragraph states the composition's thesis. What exactly is a thesis?

ANSWER: A *thesis* expresses the writer's specific viewpoint on the topic of the composition. Take the topic of advertisements, for example. Many different theses can be written about this one topic.

ONE TOPIC	MANY POSSIBLE THESIS STATEMENTS
advertisements	Whether we like it or not, advertisements are inescapable and intrusive; some are actually misleading.
	Advertisements range from the serious to the comic to the ridiculous.
	Any advertisement has two basic goals: to convince viewers they have a need, and to convince viewers to meet this need with a particular product or service.
	Advertisements can cost anything from a few dollars to many thousands of dollars.

Because one topic can inspire numerous thesis statements, an introductory paragraph cannot merely identify a topic. It must also specify the writer's approach to the topic—the thesis.

The following introductory paragraph is complete except for a thesis, which belongs where the blank is. What would be a good thesis for this paragraph?

Many forms of poetry exist, appealing to different tastes in readers. Some readers are drawn to the beauty of poetry and to its ability to express unforgettable ideas in a few choice words. But what about readers who prefer something more lighthearted and entertaining? The genre has much to offer them, too. _____ Any reader in search of poetic delight is sure to find it in one of these forms.

QUESTIONS: Which two choices below would each be a strong thesis statement for the above paragraph? Which two would be weak thesis statements? Why?

CHOICE 1: Keep reading to find out what forms are humorous and witty.

CHOICE 2: Readers should turn to a grue, a concrete poem, or a limerick.

CHOICE 3: A few fun and humorous poets are Lewis Carroll, Ogden Nash, and Edward Gorey.

CHOICE 4: Fun forms of poetry, including the grue, the concrete poem, and the limerick, celebrate dark humor, visual whimsy, and witty rhymes.

ANSWERS: Choices 2 and 4 would each be a strong thesis in the above paragraph. Both of them narrow the topic of poetry to three specific forms. In doing so, they let readers know that the composition will have three main points: the grue, the concrete poem, and the limerick. Choice 2, the simpler of the two, simply specifies the three forms. Choice 4 goes a step farther and identifies each form's type of humor.

Choices 1 and 3 would each be poor thesis statements. Choice 1 offers no new information. Instead of saying something specific about the topic of poetry, it tells readers to "keep reading." No one who reads this thesis knows what to expect from the composition. Choice 3 goes off topic by naming poets. Remember that the topic of the composition is poetry, so the thesis should state something specific about poetry.

ACTIVITY 1

Decide which sentence (A, B, or C) would make the best thesis for the following introductory paragraph. Write the letter of your choice on the blank and then explain why it is a good thesis.

Observant drivers may have noticed a new road sign in our town. It says "Littering is unlAWFUL." If you have ever tossed a bottle, soda can, candy wrapper, or cigarette butt out your car window, then this sign means YOU. Littering our streets and roads is indeed awful.

Choices:

A. Litter looks trashy, it requires paid personnel to clean it up, and it sends a message that our citizens couldn't care less about their town.

B. Anyone who litters is awful, so stop littering today.

C. Other cleanup problems in our town include overgrown parks and trails, illegally dumped refuse, and dog excrement left on lawns.

THESIS: _____

WHY IT IS GOOD: _____

_____

_____

QUESTION: How can I write a strong thesis?

ANSWER: Complete the following four steps.

STEPS TO WRITING A STRONG THESIS	EXAMPLES
Prewriting (1) Identify the topic. (2) List specific details about the topic.	*dogs* *There are small dogs and big dogs. Dogs make good pets. Small breeds include the Chihuahua, the toy poodle, and the Tibetan spaniel.*
Drafting (3) Take a specific viewpoint or position on your topic. (4) Use the topic and the details to write a statement of your viewpoint—the thesis.	*Small dogs make good indoor pets.* ***Small dogs such as the Chihuahua, the toy poodle, and the Tibetan spaniel make wonderful indoor pets.***

Study this additional example of the development of a thesis.

1. Identify the topic. *scholarships*

2. List specific details about the topic. *They help students in financial need. Different kinds of scholarships exist, such as those for sports, academics, and financial need. Without a scholarship, some students would have to drop out of college.*

3. Take a specific viewpoint or position on the topic: *Scholarships provide a way to stay in college even if the student cannot afford to pay tuition.*

4. Use the topic and the details to write a complete sentence—the thesis. **Scholarships help students in financial need attend college instead of dropping out.**

ACTIVITY 2

Complete each step to write a thesis about the given topic.

1. Identify the topic. *football season*

2. List specific details about the topic.

_____

_____

_____

3. Take a viewpoint or position.

_____

_____

_____

4. Use the topic and the details to write a complete sentence—the thesis.

_____

_____

_____

ACTIVITY 3

Complete each step to write a thesis about the given topic.

1. Identify the topic. *minimum wage*

2. List specific details about the topic.

_____

_____

_____

3. Take a viewpoint or position.

_____

_____

_____

4. Use the topic and the details to write a complete sentence—the thesis.

_____

_____

_____

ACTIVITY 4 _____

Complete each step to write a thesis about the given topic.

1. Identify the topic. _respect_

2. List specific details about the topic.

_____

_____

_____

3. Take a viewpoint or position.

_____

_____

_____

4. Use the topic and the details to write a complete sentence—the thesis.

_____

_____

_____

ACTIVITY 5 _____

Complete each step to write a thesis about the given topic.

1. Identify the topic. _fund-raisers_

2. List specific details about the topic.

_____

_____

_____

3. Take a viewpoint or position.

_____

_____

_____

4. Use the topic and the details to write a complete sentence—the thesis.

_____

_____

_____

When writing a thesis, make sure that it does not merely state a basic fact or a topic. To be meaty enough to fuel an entire composition, a thesis must require explanation or proof. Recall the sample thesis about small dogs. Suppose the thesis had been written like this:

The Chihuahua, the toy poodle, and the Tibetan spaniel are small dogs.

This sentence identifies a topic and includes specific details, but it does not state a viewpoint or position on small dogs. It merely states a fact. For this reason, it would not work as the thesis of a composition.

Here are additional examples of weak and strong thesis sentences.

WEAK: Ulysses S. Grant was a general in the Civil War.

(This sentence merely states a fact. It does not form the basis for an entire composition.)

STRONG: The Union's victory in the Civil War was due to the leadership of General Ulysses S. Grant.

(This thesis states a viewpoint about Grant that the writer can prove with reasons and examples. This thesis is meaty enough to fuel a complete essay.)

STRONG: As a general in the Civil War, Ulysses S. Grant gained success by being open-minded to new battle techniques and by learning from his mistakes.

(This thesis states specifically how Grant gained success, and with this thesis, the writer can develop an essay using supporting examples.)

WEAK: Some people feel too frightened to give a speech in public.

(This sentence gives information but does not express a point of view.)

STRONG: Joining a debate club can help those with a fear of public speaking to break through that fear.

(This thesis states a specific viewpoint about fear of public speaking.)

WEAK: Sooner or later, all friends argue.

(This statement leaves readers wondering, "So what?")

STRONG: Sooner or later all friends argue, but by following a few guidelines for fighting fairly, they can strengthen, not lose, their friendship.

(This thesis expresses the writer's specific viewpoint on the topic of arguments between friends. It tells readers that the writer will explain guidelines for fighting fairly.)

ACTIVITY 6

Improve each thesis by rewriting it to state a specific viewpoint or position on the topic.

> **Samples:**
>
> **a.** In some households, the television is on for more than four hours every day.
>
> *The right hobby can prove more interesting than the average television show.*
>
> **b.** Not everyone goes by his or her given name but goes by a nickname instead.
>
> *People's nicknames are clues to how their families perceive them.*

1. The mouse and the gerbil are small, furry rodents.

   _____

   _____

2. Bad habits are hard to break.

   _____

   _____

3. A full-time job typically consists of forty hours per week.

   _____

   _____

4. Some teachers give a lot of homework.

   _____

   _____

5. Mosquitoes are pests.

   _____

   _____

QUESTION: Where does the thesis go in the introductory paragraph?

ANSWER: The thesis can come at any place in the introductory paragraph. However, a reliable strategy is to include the thesis as the last, or next to last, sentence in the introduction. With this structure, the sentences build from general to specific. In particular, the first sentence or two identify the topic of the composition. The next few sentences hook the reader's interest in the topic. Last, the thesis states the writer's specific viewpoint on the topic.

Recall the introductory paragraph about advertisements.

[1]Advertising is big business, helping companies to attract new customers and keep the ones they already have. [2]In fact, the advertisement industry seems to know just where we, the consumers, are, and how to get their ads in front of our faces. [3]Advertisements, also called commercials, are talented shape-shifters, appearing in print, on television, and on the Web. [4]Consequently, encountering ads is a fact of life. [5]Whether we like it or not, advertisements are inescapable and intrusive; some are actually misleading.

In this paragraph, the sentences progress from general to specific.

S1 identifies the general topic, advertisements.

S2–S4 narrow the topic, giving readers an idea of the composition's approach to advertisements. These sentences offer details that hook readers' interest, causing them to continue reading.

S5, the thesis, states a specific viewpoint on advertisements. This sentence limits the composition to the discussion of three main qualities of advertisements.

Now look at the introductory paragraph about forms of poetry. These sentences, too, progress from general to specific. However, the thesis sentence is next to last instead of last.

[1]Many forms of poetry exist, appealing to different tastes in readers. [2]Some readers are drawn to the beauty of poetry and to its ability to express unforgettable ideas in a few choice words. [3]But what about readers who prefer something more lighthearted and entertaining? [4]The genre has much to offer them, too. [5]Fun forms of poetry, including the grue, the concrete poem, and the limerick, celebrate dark humor, visual whimsy, and witty rhymes. [6]Any reader in search of poetic delight is sure to find it in one of these forms.

This format works just as well. In this case, the final sentence (S6) emphasizes the value of finding out the details that the thesis (S5) promises.

Choose one of the thesis statements you wrote in Activities 2–6 and use it to write an introductory paragraph. Build your sentences from general to specific, placing your thesis last or next to last. Before you get started, read the sample paragraph and comments below.

Sample Paragraph:

[1]In the United States, education through high school is free to every citizen. [2]When it comes to higher education, however, many students hit a roadblock: cash. [3]They wonder how they can get the money for tuition, fees, and books. [4]These charges can add up to thousands of dollars every semester. [5]Faced with this price tag, some students simply do not go to college, or they drop out. [6]But have they truly pursued every option for staying in school? [7]Scholarships help students in financial need attend college instead of dropping out.

Comments: In this paragraph, the sentences progress from general to specific.

S1 and S2 identify the general topic, paying for a college education.

S3–S5 narrow the topic, focusing on specific costs and students' responses to paying them.

S6 points readers' attention to S7, the thesis: *Scholarships help students in financial need attend college instead of dropping out.*

Now, write your own introductory paragraph on a separate sheet of paper. Underline the thesis sentence.

Conclusion Paragraphs

A composition begins with an introduction, followed by body paragraphs (the kinds of paragraphs you wrote in Lessons 13 and 14 are typical of body paragraphs). A *conclusion paragraph* gives closure to a composition by driving home the paper's main idea, or thesis. It comes last in the composition, but it is just as important as the introductory paragraph. Why? It is the final paragraph your audience reads before putting down the composition, and it is the perfect opportunity to drive home your thesis.

 The *conclusion paragraph,* usually the last paragraph of a composition, drives home the main idea of the composition.

Read this example of a conclusion paragraph:

[1]Clearly, the inescapable, intrusive, and misleading nature of advertisements confronts virtually all of us. [2]These ads invade all media, from radio to television to print to the Internet. [3]Frequently unwelcome and often misleading, they are an unavoidable irritation. [4]However, advertisements are not all-powerful. [5]An informed consumer who understands the nature of advertisements can turn the page or glance away and refuse to fall for false promises.

This conclusion paragraph has three main parts.

S1 restates the thesis of the composition. This sentence signals readers that the composition is coming to an end. No new examples or reasons will be presented after this point.

S2 and S3 summarize key ideas from body paragraphs, which support the thesis.

S4 and S5 bring everything to a close by telling readers why the composition's main points are valuable or useful. In particular, readers of this composition have the knowledge they need to reject unwelcome advertisements.

Notice that the conclusion does not repeat the introductory paragraph, nor does it repeat the thesis verbatim (word-for-word).

The length of a conclusion paragraph is determined by the length of the entire composition. The conclusion paragraph of a short essay (say, three or four paragraphs) can establish closure with just a few sentences. A longer essay (say, eight to ten paragraphs) may require a slightly longer conclusion in order to bring the discussion to a close. In both short and longer conclusions, though, the primary task is to bring closure to the composition, not to recap every main point.

QUESTION: Are conclusion paragraphs truly necessary?

ANSWER: Without a conclusion, a composition would end abruptly. Readers would likely wonder, "Is that all? Did I reach the end?" They might even look for another paragraph, wondering how to tie together all the ideas raised in support of the thesis.

Read this short composition, which lacks a conclusion.

Grues and Concrete Poems: Fun Forms of Poetry

Many forms of poetry exist, appealing to different tastes in readers. Some readers are drawn to the beauty-inspiring nature of poetry. But what about readers who prefer something more lighthearted and entertaining? The genre has much to offer them, too. Two fun forms of poetry, the grue and the concrete poem, celebrate dark humor and visual whimsy.

Short for *gruesome,* the grue celebrates ghastly subject matter in a witty manner. Writers of grues spin rhymes about unlucky accidents, unfortunate endings, and unlawful actions. Dreadful acts and accidents abound in these poems, but always with a comic twist. Not to be taken literally, these gruesome rhymes are simply a cheeky form of entertainment.

The appeal of a concrete poem is its shape, for its lines are arranged so that, taken together, they form the shape of an object. One popular shape is a Christmas tree. The first line is very short and centered. Line 2 is a bit longer and centered under line 1. Each successive line is longer, forming the shape of a triangle with a little "trunk"—a Christmas tree. Other popular shapes/topics for concrete poems are a kite, a snake, a heart, and a raindrop.

QUESTIONS: Which of the following two paragraphs would be a strong conclusion to the composition on page 142? Which would be a weak conclusion? Why?

CHOICE 1: [1]Clearly, the grue and the concrete poem are fun forms of poetry that offer dark humor and visual whimsy. [2]In a witty manner, grues describe ghastly subjects and poke fun at them to make them less scary. [3]Concrete poems have lines arranged to form the shape of an object such as a Christmas tree. [4]These are fun forms of poetry for readers who prefer something lighthearted and entertaining.

CHOICE 2: [1]Readers looking for lighthearted fun are sure to enjoy the comic horrors in grues and the eye-catching shapes of concrete poems. [2]By poking fun at potentially disturbing subjects, grues provide healthy comic relief. [3]Concrete poems, by presenting ideas in fetching shapes, entice readers to find joy in an idea's visual presentation. [4]Together, these fun poetic forms meet the needs of readers seeking cheer.

ANSWERS: Choice 2 would be a strong conclusion to the composition. S1 restates the thesis using fresh words that refer to details in the body of the composition. S2 and S3 summarize the main points in the body paragraphs. S4 ties everything together in a final statement on the value of grues and concrete poems.

Choice 1 would be a weak conclusion to the composition. At first glance, it contains all the essential parts. However, each sentence merely repeats a previous sentence in the composition nearly verbatim. S1 repeats the thesis, S2 repeats the topic sentence of the first body paragraph, and S3 repeats the topic sentence of the second body paragraph. S4 repeats the second sentence in the introductory paragraph. As a result, this conclusion paragraph sounds repetitive and formulaic.

QUESTION: Do certain words signal a conclusion?

ANSWER: Yes, certain words and expressions signal a conclusion. They include *in summary, to sum up, finally, in conclusion, for these reasons, to conclude, on the whole, in general,* and *after all.* However, many—if not most—conclusions are successful without such signal phrases.

ACTIVITY 8

Write a suitable conclusion paragraph for the following composition, "Responsibilities of Friendship." Be sure to include the three main parts of a conclusion:

1. a restatement, in fresh words, of the thesis

2. a summary of the main points in the body paragraphs

3. a statement about why the composition's information is valuable or useful

After reading the composition that follows, write your conclusion paragraph on a separate sheet of paper.

Responsibilities of Friendship

Most people would agree that friendship is one of the best parts of life. Most people have one or two good friends, and others have even more. No matter how many friends you have, however, one truth is unavoidable. Friendship carries the responsibilities of faithfulness and honesty.

A faithful friend is loyal to you no matter what. For example, if she hears a rumor that you said something nasty about her, she comes to you for the truth rather than believing the rumor. If you tell your friend a secret, he does not blab it or even "accidentally" leak it. Above all, a faithful friend remains loyal even if you go through rough patches when you disagree or fight. When the dust settles, your friend is still there.

Even more important, a true friend is honest. Honesty shows respect to the other person. When a friend truly respects you, she will tell you the truth, even if the truth is difficult. In addition, honesty in a friend shows a willingness to put you first. In contrast, someone who lies is thinking only of himself and what is easiest to say. No matter what else friends may have going for them, a friendship cannot last without honesty.

Arranging Paragraphs in a Composition

The paragraphs in a composition are arranged in a specific order.

1. introductory paragraph
2. body paragraphs
3. conclusion paragraph

Study the following sample composition, "The Nature of Advertisements." It illustrates the typical structure of a composition. Notice how ideas and information are organized within the paragraphs. Notice, too, how the introduction informs readers of the thesis and how the conclusion drives home the thesis and gives closure.

The Nature of Advertisements

Advertising is big business, helping companies to attract new customers and keep the ones they already have. In fact, the advertisement industry seems to know just where we, the consumers, are, and how to get their ads in front of our faces. Advertisements, also called commercials, are talented shape-shifters, appearing in print, on television, and on the Web. Consequently, encountering ads is a fact of life. Whether we like it or not, advertisements are inescapable and intrusive; some are actually misleading.

This paragraph is the paper's introduction. It begins by identifying the topic in a general way (advertisements). Then it narrows the topic to certain qualities of ads, hooking the reader's interest. The last sentence states the thesis.

No matter what you do or where you go, businesses confront you with commercials. Are you watching television? Expect plenty of "special messages from our sponsors." Are you listening to the radio? Be prepared for your favorite songs to be "coming right up after these words from local businesses." As you drive along the streets of town, billboards and business signs compete for your attention. The bus in front of you may display an advertisement on its back or sides. Is there any way to escape the bombardment of advertising?

Many people hoped that the World Wide Web would be a fun place to cruise around, reading and chatting, without worrying about advertisements cropping up every two seconds. But as any Internet surfer knows, ad banners have become a fact of life. They pop up nearly everywhere you go on the Net, whether to a merchant site, a news site, or even a page of search results. Not only that, but businesses inundate your e-mail account with unsolicited sales pitches, otherwise known as spam. Advertising, it seems, is here to stay, whether in traditional venues like billboards or in the newer venues of technology.

Many advertisements promise more than the product can realistically deliver. For example, some ads make viewers think that eating a certain brand of potato chips is an exciting and happy experience. In the ads, people sing and dance and toss chips into one another's mouths. Everyone seems incredibly carefree, attractive, and healthy, as though these potato chips have made every dream come true. The message: Eat these chips and your life will be complete!

Well, I am here to tell you that eating potato chips—of any brand—does not solve life's problems. In fact, it can create problems. For example, eating potato chips can make you gain weight because they are high in fat. Eating chips can also put your health at risk because chips are not a healthful food. If you eat them instead of a healthful snack, you deprive your body of needed nutrients. Finally, if you eat chips in hopes of chasing away unhappiness, you will be disappointed. Potato chips do not solve emotional problems.

Clearly, the inescapable, intrusive, and misleading nature of advertisements confronts virtually all of us. These ads invade all media, from radio to television to print to the Internet. Frequently unwelcome and often misleading, they are an unavoidable irritation. However, advertisements are not all-powerful. An informed consumer who understands the nature of advertisements can turn the page or glance away and refuse to fall for false promises.

This body paragraph begins with a topic sentence that links to the first point in the thesis: ads are inescapable. The other sentences give supporting details. Since every detail supports the main idea, the paragraph is unified. The final sentence builds a bridge to the next paragraph.

This paragraph begins with a topic sentence that responds to the question in the previous paragraph. The other sentences provide support by explaining that Web ads can be intrusive. The entire paragraph develops the second point in the thesis.

A topic sentence begins the paragraph, supporting the third point in the paper's thesis: ads can be misleading. Notice that the writer does more than just say that ads are misleading—she gives specific supporting details to show how they mislead.

A topic sentence begins the paragraph, building on the topic of the previous paragraph. The transitions In fact, For example, and Finally help unify the paragraph. All the sentences support the topic sentence by providing specific details.

This conclusion paragraph gives closure by restating the thesis, summing up key ideas, and emphasizing the value of the information.

Recall these elements of a strong paragraph:
- appropriate length
- unity
- topic sentence (in body paragraphs)
- well-developed reasons or examples that support the topic sentence, arranged in a logical sequence
- clincher sentence, if appropriate

ACTIVITY 1 _____

Some of the following paragraphs have unity; some do not. Identify which sentences are off topic, or write *none* if no sentence is off topic.

> **Sample:**
>
> ¹Billiards is a game requiring a special table, a set of balls, and cue sticks. ²The table is twice as long as it is wide, and it has a smooth, felt-covered surface. ³The table may or may not have pockets. ⁴Carom billiards, one version of the game, is played on a table with no pockets. ⁵Another version of the game, pool, is played on a table with six pockets. ⁶The cue sticks, typically made of polished wood, are from 40 to 60 inches long. ⁷They are used to strike the cue ball. ⁸The balls themselves, which are very hard plastic, are either 2¼ or 2⅜ inches in diameter.
>
> SENTENCES OFF TOPIC, IF ANY: _____ 4 and 5 _____

1. ¹Keeping track of assignments, chores, and events is not difficult. ²All you need is a small planning calendar. ³Ideally, it should have space to write several notations for each day. ⁴To keep track of your schedule, simply write an appointment, etc., on the appropriate day of the calendar. ⁵If necessary, record a time (such as 10:00 A.M.). ⁶To avoid confusion, note *all* events in this *one* calendar. ⁷Using this method, you can keep your life on track.

   SENTENCES OFF TOPIC, IF ANY: _____

2. ¹Acupuncture is a method of preventing and relieving pain. ²To treat a person, an acupuncturist inserts hair-thin needles into specific spots on the body, called acupuncture points. ³When choosing an acupuncturist, find out if he or she has been properly trained. ⁴Different points correspond to pain relief for different parts of the body. ⁵The technician then gently stimulates the needles by twirling or by using heat, electricity, or another method. ⁶For many, acupuncture is the perfect antidote to pain. ⁷Other treatments for pain include ice packs, heating pads, and medication.

   SENTENCES OFF TOPIC, IF ANY: _____

3. [1]Instead of relying on vending machines to meet your snack needs, pack your own healthful snacks. [2]Prices for vending machine snacks range from a couple of quarters to a dollar or more. [3]You can easily carry plastic bags of dried fruit, nuts, or granola in your book bag, briefcase, or purse. [4]Simply prepare a few bags each weekend and reach for them throughout the week. [5]One of my favorite childhood snacks was a kind of candy "rock" that fizzled and popped in my mouth. [6]With these snacks on hand, you are less likely to resort to the sugary items in vending machines.

SENTENCES OFF TOPIC, IF ANY: _____

ACTIVITY 2 _____

Write topic sentences that follow the instructions below.

> **Samples:**
>
> **a.** Write a topic sentence for a paragraph about weather.
>
> The unpredictable danger of tornadoes attracts people called storm chasers.
>
> **b.** Write a topic sentence for a paragraph that tells why anger is healthy.
>
> Holding anger inside results in pent-up fury, but expressing anger brings
>
> peace of mind.

1. Write a topic sentence for a paragraph that tells why you like a certain song.

   _____

   _____

2. Write a topic sentence for a paragraph about nicknames.

   _____

   _____

3. Write a topic sentence for a paragraph about beauty.

   _____

   _____

4. Write a topic sentence for a paragraph about UFOs (unidentified flying objects).

   _____

   _____

5. Write a topic sentence about a specific school rule.

   _____

   _____

Decide which sentence (A, B, or C) would make the best clincher sentence for the following paragraph. Write the letter of your choice on the blank and then explain why it is a good clincher sentence.

Sample:

Fall is the season I enjoy most. It is a pleasure to be outdoors in the fall because there are few mosquitoes and the weather is mild. The colorful autumn leaves make the outdoors more beautiful. When I finish classes on a fall day, I can't wait to get out on the hockey field or just take my time walking home with friends. I always feel better and have more energy in the fall than in any other season.

Choices:

A. After autumn, my next favorite season is summer.

B. If it were up to me, I would have nothing but fall all year round.

C. One fun fall activity is raking leaves into a pile and then jumping into the pile.

CLINCHER SENTENCE: ___B___

WHY IT IS GOOD: This sentence emphasizes how much the writer loves fall, which is the main idea of the paragraph.

People who have never been to a state fair are missing out on an amazing experience. For one thing, the games and rides are a thrill for visitors of any age. After a few rides, fair-goers can rest while eating caramel corn, hot dogs, or corn on the cob. Then they can walk through the animal exhibits and see prize-winning pigs, heifers, lambs, and goats.

Choices:

A. The games and rides are truly the best part of the state fair.

B. Many people enjoy the performances by local singers and dancers.

C. Experiencing these and other state fair activities makes the day unforgettable.

CLINCHER SENTENCE: _____

WHY IT IS GOOD: _____

_____

_____

Write a suitable clincher sentence for the following paragraph. Then tell why it is a good one.

Amelia Earhart had a brief but remarkable career in aviation. In 1932, she became the first woman to fly alone across the Atlantic. Three years later, she flew from Hawaii to California by herself. No one had ever done that before. In 1937, with copilot Frederick J. Noonan, she tried to fly around the world, but her plane disappeared in the middle of the Pacific. No trace of it—or her—was ever found.

CLINCHER SENTENCE: _____

_____

_____

WHY IT IS GOOD: _____

_____

_____

ACTIVITY 5 _____

Each topic sentence below can be developed into a paragraph by using examples or reasons. Two examples or reasons are listed. Add a third.

Samples:

a. TOPIC SENTENCE: Learning a second language has several benefits.

EXAMPLES:
- **1.** It qualifies you for additional job opportunities.
- **2.** It is helpful for international travel.
- **3.** It opens up new possibilities for friendships.

b. TOPIC SENTENCE: The new "green homes" are the best choice for new homeowners.

REASONS:
- **1.** They use less energy for heating and cooling.
- **2.** They are constructed of earth-friendly materials.
- **3.** They are affordable to build or buy.

1. TOPIC SENTENCE: A car owner must pay for certain routine expenses.

EXAMPLES:
- **1.** She must buy car insurance.
- **2.** She must change the oil regularly.
- **3.** _____

2. TOPIC SENTENCE: Life in a big city is not ideal for everyone.

REASONS:
- **1.** The noise of cars, trains, airplanes, and alarms can be stressful.
- **2.** Living in a sea of strangers can be lonely.
- **3.** _____

3. TOPIC SENTENCE: The ocean is filled with fascinating creatures.

    EXAMPLES: **1.** the blowfish

                 2. the stingray

                 3. _____

4. TOPIC SENTENCE: Mr. Majors deserves the Teacher of the Year award.

    REASONS: **1.** He sponsors three different student clubs.

                 2. He attends all his students' sports games.

                 3. _____

5. TOPIC SENTENCE: An effective apology has three essential parts.

    EXAMPLES: **1.** sincerity

                 2. an admission of guilt

                 3. _____

 Writing Application

Writing a Well-Developed Paragraph

Choose one of the following topics and write a paragraph about it. Be sure to include a topic sentence and well-developed examples or reasons, arranged logically. Include a clincher sentence, if appropriate. Write your paragraph on a separate sheet of paper.

Suggested Topics

extreme sports	shoplifting	curfews	surprise parties
sibling rivalry	homework	stereotypes	public speaking

Recall these parts of a strong introductory paragraph:
- identification of the composition's topic
- narrowing of the topic to one specific idea
- expression of the main idea in a thesis

ACTIVITY 6

Decide which sentence (A, B, or C) would make the best thesis for the following introductory paragraph. Write the letter of your choice on the blank and then explain why it is a good thesis.

Some people keep a lucky penny in their pocket, hoping it will cause fate to smile upon them. Others carry a lucky rabbit's foot, or they hang a horseshoe over their front door. Still others search for a lucky four-leaf clover or wear their lucky shirt to take a test. These and other so-called good-luck charms are popular with children and adults alike. But do they really work? *(Thesis belongs here.)*

Choices:

A. Several recent studies show surprising links between good-luck charms and the kind of luck the charm's owner has.

B. Similar to good-luck charms are fortune cookies, which offer a prediction or advice regarding the recipient's fortune.

C. Some people do not believe in fate, while others not only believe but also try to alter its course.

THESIS: _____

WHY IT IS GOOD: _____

_____

_____

ACTIVITY 7 _____

Complete each step to write a thesis about the given topic.

1. Identify the topic. *ending a friendship*

2. List specific details about the topic.

    _____

    _____

    _____

3. Use the topic and the details to write a thesis sentence.

    _____

    _____

    _____

ACTIVITY 8 _____

Complete each step to write a thesis about the given topic.

1. Identify the topic. *physical fitness*

2. List specific details about the topic.

    _____

    _____

    _____

3. Use the topic and the details to write a thesis sentence.

_____

_____

_____

 Writing
Application   Write an Introductory Paragraph

Choose one of the thesis statements you wrote in Activities 7 and 8, and use it to write an introductory paragraph. Build your sentences from general to specific, placing your thesis last or next to last. Write your paragraph on a separate sheet of paper.

Recall these parts of a strong conclusion paragraph:
- restatement of the thesis
- summary of key ideas
- final emphasis on value of composition's content

 Writing
Application   Write a Conclusion Paragraph

Read the introductory paragraph you wrote in the previous Writing Application. Next, list three main points that would develop and support this thesis in a composition (for examples of such a list, see Activity 6). Finally, write a conclusion paragraph that restates the thesis in fresh words, summarizes the key ideas, and emphasizes the value of the information.

Paragraph Composition

The following research applications encourage you to take your **paragraph composition** beyond this workbook and into real life. Each assignment asks you to gather information on one of the themes in the previous lessons and to write strong paragraphs about your findings. Enjoy your research and take pride in using your skills of paragraph composition!

THEME: Advertising

SKILL: Writing Paragraphs

Sooner or later, most people desire an expensive item such as a leather coat, designer sunglasses, a mountain bike, a big TV, etc. Choose one costly item that interests you and research advertisements for it. Specifically, evaluate at least **five** ads for "truth in advertising." For example, an ad for a leather coat that tells size, materials, stitching style, number of pockets, etc., is helpful and informative. An ad that suggests the leather coat will make you popular is misleading.

As you research various ads, take notes on details related to truth in advertising. Then write two paragraphs about your findings. For example, your first paragraph could tell how ads for your chosen item can be helpful and truthful, while the second paragraph tells how ads for the item can be misleading.

THEME: Politics

SKILL: Writing Unified Paragraphs

Learning about politics involves asking questions and finding answers. For example, here are three questions that someone might ask:

How do I register to vote?

Who are my state senators, and how can I contact them?

What is one important issue up for vote in my town or city?

Choose one of these questions and then find information with which to form an answer. Useful sources to research are federal, state, and city government Web sites; local newspapers; and school newsletters, newspapers, and Web sites. Gather enough information to write a two-paragraph answer to your chosen question. This means sticking to the basics and organizing the information in a logical, easy-to-follow way.

Finally, write your paragraphs and edit them to ensure each is unified.

THEME: Leaders

SKILL: Writing Topic Sentences

Like Martin Luther King, Jr., many people have taken risks to support a cause in which they believe. Here are just a few names:

Sally Ride	Gloria Steinem	John Glenn
Tecumseh	Jane Goodall	Clara Barton
Gandhi	Malcolm X	Cesar Chavez

Choose one of the people listed on page 153, or another public figure you know about, and find out about his or her achievements. Helpful sources include encyclopedia articles, biographies, interviews, speeches, and chapters or articles in larger works (online or in print).

Next, narrow down the information to an idea about which you can write **two** paragraphs. Finally, write your paragraphs. Make sure each one has a topic sentence that identifies the main idea of the paragraph, and underline this sentence. Make sure each sentence in the paragraph explains or proves the topic sentence.

THEME: Poetry

SKILL: Writing Paragraphs With Clincher Sentences

Many forms of poetry exist, appealing to different tastes in readers. In fact, a person who normally does not like poetry may be intrigued, nevertheless, by a grue, a concrete poem, or a limerick.

From the list below, choose a form of poetry to research. Find out what the distinguishing characteristics of the type are, along with the names of at least two poets who have written in that style.

Styles:

ballad	limerick	pastoral
blank verse	lyric poetry	sonnet
elegy	nursery rhyme	villanelle
free verse	ode	

Then write **two** paragraphs explaining the information you find out. Make sure each paragraph has a clincher sentence that drives home the point of the topic sentence, and underline this clincher sentence.

THEME: Information

SKILL: Developing Paragraphs With Examples

At the top of a sheet of paper, write the phrase *So you want to . . .*

Underneath, brainstorm a list of activities and projects you would like to do but don't know how to do. Examples are *become a professional basketball player, build a jewelry box, buy a used car that's not a lemon,* and so on. For other ideas, type "So you want to" into an Internet search engine and see what comes up.

Choose one activity or project and research exactly how to accomplish it. Then write **two or three** paragraphs that give the essential information. For instance, you might divide the entire process into two or three main stages, with each stage being the topic of one paragraph. Be sure to develop your examples fully and arrange them in a logical order.

THEME: Persuasion

SKILL: Developing Paragraphs With Reasons

Choose a controversial topic that interests you and find out more about it. Examples are, banning smoking in restaurants, mandatory drug testing for employment applications, capital punishment (the death penalty), a specific minority's rights, and so on. Note that each of these suggestions is only a topic. You must develop a point of view about the topic or decide on an action you think readers should take.

Using your research, brainstorm a list of reasons why readers should accept your point of view or call to action. Then write **two** paragraphs of about seven or eight sentences each. Develop each paragraph with reasons arranged to build up to the strongest. For example, if you are writing about banning smoking in restaurants, paragraph 1 may persuade readers that such a ban is a good idea, and paragraph 2 may persuade readers to show their support of the ban by taking one or more actions (writing a city council member, writing an opinion piece for the newspaper, etc.).

Paragraph Composition

Directions: The following passage is the draft of a composition. The sentences are numbered for ease of reference. Some parts of the passage need to be revised. Read the passage and circle the letter of the best answer to each question and write it on the blank. If the best answer is to leave a part unchanged, choose the letter for NO CHANGE.

Lance Armstrong: A Hero for the Right Reasons

[1]Many sports heroes are known only to followers of the sport. [2]Others, such as Olympic heroes, gain recognition because of a few moments in the national spotlight. [3]Similarly, Lance Armstrong is a different kind of sports hero.

[4]From an early age, Lance Armstrong demonstrated superior athletic ability and a competitive streak. [5]The cycling part of the triathlon became his focus, and he devoted his life to professional cycling. [6]In that sport he has excelled. [7]These qualities helped him win the Iron Kids Triathlon at age thirteen and, at age sixteen, become a professional triathlete.

[8]In October 1996, he discovered that he had testicular cancer that had advanced and spread to his brain and lungs. [9]Now, the determination that had carried him through win after win in cycling kicked in to help him combat the deadly disease. [10]And combat he did. [11]After surgery and chemotherapy, Lance became a cancer survivor. [12]To help cancer patients like Armstrong survive, some groups organize "cancer walks" to raise money and awareness. [13]Profoundly affected by his battle for life, he became a spokesperson for cancer awareness and survivorship.

[14]By committing himself from such an early age to the triathlon and to cycling, Armstrong set the stage for his own success. [15]His determination helped him reach his goals while becoming a better athlete. [16]His unwavering dedication to cycling, even after facing cancer, made him a hero to anyone who faces an overwhelming challenge.

_____ **1.** Which is the best revision of the underlined portion of sentence 3 (reproduced below)?

<u>Similarly, Lance Armstrong</u> is a different kind of sports hero.

A. NO CHANGE

B. Lance Armstrong

C. For example, Lance Armstrong

D. Lance Armstrong, therefore,

_____ **2.** Which of the following sentences would make the best thesis for the introduction paragraph, to be inserted just after sentence 3?

    F. He has earned fame and gained fans' heartfelt admiration for his amazing abilities as a triathlete and cyclist.

    G. By committing himself as a youngster to the triathlon and to cycling, he set the stage for his success.

    H. This essay will explain why Armstrong deserves our respect and admiration.

    J. He has earned fame and admiration not only for his success as a cyclist but also for his victory over cancer.

_____ **3.** Which of the following is the most well-developed version of sentence 6?

    A. NO CHANGE

    B. In that sport, he has excelled by winning various championships and other contests.

    C. In that sport he has excelled as national and world champion, as Olympian, and as six-time winner of the Tour de France.

    D. In that sport, he has won a lot of awards, which he deserves.

_____ **4.** What is the best sequence of sentences in the second paragraph?

    F. NO CHANGE

    G. 4, 7, 5, 6

    H. 5, 6, 4, 7

    J. 6, 4, 7, 5

_____ **5.** Which of the following sentences would make the best clincher sentence for the second paragraph?

    A. In these ways, he demonstrated his superior athletic abilities and competitiveness.

    B. On the other hand, he started young and remained true to his goals, which led to success.

    C. His success was probably due to a natural, inborn tendency toward excellence in sports.

    D. Clearly, he is one of the all-time great cyclists.

_____ **6.** Which of the following sentences would make the best topic sentence for the third paragraph, to be inserted just before sentence 8?

    F. His path, however, has not been without obstacles and pain.

    G. Each year in America, people are diagnosed with cancer.

    H. Life is full of surprises.

    J. We think of cancer as a smoker's disease, but cancer strikes nonsmokers, too.

_____ **7.** Which is the best revision of the underlined portion of sentence 9 (reproduced below)?

   Now, the determination that had carried him through win after win in cycling kicked in to help him combat the deadly disease.

   A. NO CHANGE

   B. As a result, the determination

   C. In addition, the determination

   D. The determination

_____ **8.** Which sentence creates a lack of unity in its paragraph?

   F. 2

   G. 5

   H. 12

   J. 14

_____ **9.** Which of the following changes to the conclusion paragraph is most needed?

   A. NO CHANGE

   B. After sentence 18, add a sentence giving examples of overwhelming challenges.

   C. After sentence 14, add a sentence listing each of Armstrong's successes.

   D. After sentence 15, add a sentence explaining exactly how Armstrong became a better athlete.

_____ **10.** Which of the following revisions to sentence 16 is most needed?

   F. NO CHANGE

   G. Add "Likewise," to the beginning of the sentence.

   H. Remove "even after facing cancer" from the sentence.

   J. Add "More important," to the beginning of the sentence.

Directions: Write a paragraph in response to the following prompt. Use the checklist for paragraph composition on pages 187–188 to plan, draft, and edit your paragraph. Use a separate sheet of paper for all prewriting and drafting; then write the final copy of the paragraph on the lines below.

> Nearly everyone enjoys indulging in at least one guilty pleasure. It may be eating cookies in bed after midnight, listening to sappy love songs at high volume, or watching Saturday-morning cartoons on TV for hours. What is your favorite guilty pleasure? Write a paragraph identifying and explaining it.

_____

_____

_____

_____

_____

_____

_____

_____

_____

_____

_____

_____

_____

_____

PART 3

Directions: Write an introduction paragraph of an essay in response to the following prompt. Use the checklist for paragraph composition on pages 187–188 to plan, draft, and edit your paragraph. Use a separate sheet of paper for all prewriting and drafting; then write the final copy of the paragraph on the lines below.

Safety issues are always a concern on school campuses. Specific issues may concern fire safety, traffic dangers, weapons, bullies, protective gear for sports, Internet safety, and more. At your school, what safety issues are most in need of improvement or updating? Write an **introduction paragraph** of an essay that persuades readers that your campus needs one or more specific safety updates.

PART

4 Paragraph Revision

In Part Three you learned the basics of composing paragraphs. Now, in Part Four, you will turn your attention to revising paragraphs to make them stronger and more effective. As with sentence revision, paragraph revision is an important step in making sure your final written product says exactly what you mean it to say. In the following lessons, we will focus on

- making the topic sentence focused and specific
- creating unity in the paragraph
- arranging the supporting sentences in the most effective order
- adding sentence variety by varying sentence beginnings and sentence types

In addition to the lessons, Part Four includes a Paragraph Revision Checklist to guide you in writing and revising paragraphs, as well as a selection of essay prompts that give you the opportunity to showcase your writing skills in full-length compositions.

17 Revising the Topic Sentence

In Lesson 11, you learned that a topic sentence in a paragraph states the main idea of that paragraph. In the paragraph below, the topic sentence is underlined.

¹<u>A drama, or play, has five main plot elements</u>. ²The first is the introduction. ³In this part of the plot, the characters and their situation become clear. ⁴Second is the rising action. ⁵During this part, a conflict or problem develops, and tension rises as the characters face obstacles to solving the conflict. ⁶The high point of the conflict is the climax, the third main plot element. ⁷At this point, the characters decide how to solve the problem. ⁸During the falling action, the fourth plot element, the characters carry out the solution. ⁹Finally, in the conclusion, the problem reaches resolution, and the story ends.

In this paragraph, the topic sentence (S1) pinpoints the precise idea that the paragraph discusses: *A drama, or play, has five main plot elements.* The supporting sentences explain the five elements.

S2–S3 tell about the introduction.

S4–S5 tell about the rising action.

S6–S7 tell about the high point, or climax.

S8 tells about the falling action.

S9 tells about the conclusion, or resolution.

QUESTION: What makes this topic sentence strong and effective?

ANSWER: The topic sentence expresses one specific idea that can be explained in one paragraph, and the idea is exactly what the supporting sentences discuss.

QUESTION: How can I revise a topic sentence to make it strong and effective?

ANSWER: Correct weaknesses in a topic sentence by revising it using the following checklist:

Revise the topic sentence to make sure it is
- specific, not vague
- focused, not broad
- in agreement with supporting sentences, not off topic

Let's look more closely at each of the three weaknesses listed in the revision checklist.

1. The topic sentence is vague.

A vague topic sentence leaves readers wondering what the main idea truly is. To be effective, the topic sentence must use precise word choices to express a specific, focused idea. Consider the following examples.

VAGUE: Conflict is important in a play.

(What kind of conflict? What makes the conflict important? How exactly should *important* be defined?)

SPECIFIC: The problem that characters must solve drives forward a play's plot.

(*The problem that characters must solve* is much more specific than *conflict*. Similarly, *drives forward a play's plot* makes clear *how* the conflict is "important." These precise expressions create a specific, focused topic sentence.)

VAGUE: In a play, some of the dialogue helps the audience understand the main problem.

(What part of the dialogue? In what way does the dialogue help the audience understand the problem?)

SPECIFIC: Arguments among characters in a play reveal details of the main problem to the audience.

(*Arguments among characters* is more specific than *some of the dialogue*. Likewise, *reveal details* is more precise than *help . . . understand*. Together, these expressions state a tightly focused main idea that the rest of the paragraph can support with examples.)

VAGUE: Suspense comes from the conflict and the characters.

(What aspects of "the conflict" and "the characters" produce suspense?)

SPECIFIC: The characters' struggle to solve the problem in spite of powerful opposition builds suspense.

(*The characters' struggle to solve the problem* is more specific than *the characters*. This idea of the struggle, combined with *in spite of powerful opposition,* is more specific than *the conflict*. In addition, *builds* is more specific than *comes from*.)

ACTIVITY 1

On the lines provided, rewrite each topic sentence to be more specific. Use your own knowledge and imagination to provide the specifics necessary to your revision.

Sample:

Knowing things about plays helps you enjoy watching plays.

Knowing basic dramatic concepts helps you enjoy watching a play built upon

these concepts.

Here is an alternate revision.

Knowing the typical structure of plays helps you enjoy watching this structure

unfold on stage.

1. Costumes are important to the characters.

_____

_____

2. Certain things make a play memorable.

_____

_____

3. There are different kinds of conflict.

_____

_____

4. The introduction gets the play off to a good start.

_____

_____

5. Stage directions affect the play.

_____

_____

 Writing
Application

Recognizing Vagueness
in a Topic Sentence

Think about a play (or a film) you have seen recently. In particular, think about elements of the play, such as plot, character, dialogue, props, costumes, etc. What element was especially effective or strong? To develop your ideas, brainstorm details on a separate sheet of paper.

Next, write a paragraph of about **six to eight** sentences explaining which element was strong, and why. Revise your topic sentence to make it as specific and focused as possible.

With your teacher's approval, exchange paragraphs with a classmate. In the paragraph you receive, underline the topic sentence. Then examine the topic sentence. Is it as focused and specific as it could be? If you think so, write your classmate a note explaining what makes the topic sentence specific as opposed to vague. If the topic sentence is vague, revise it to be more specific and explain why you made the changes.

Finally, share the results with your classmate.

2. The topic sentence is too broad.

If the topic sentence is too broad, the paragraph will have to be extremely long to develop the idea fully. To be effective, the topic sentence must make a statement that can be adequately supported in one paragraph.

BROAD: Thornton Wilder's play *Our Town* is renowned for its lack of stage props and its bittersweet portrayal of middle-class America.

(As a whole, this sentence states what *Our Town* is famous for. However, each point named—the lack of props and the bittersweet portrayal—needs its own set of supporting examples. A paragraph that included all this information would be long and unwieldy.)

SPECIFIC: Thornton Wilder's play *Our Town* is renowned, in part, for its lack of stage props.

(This sentence focuses tightly on one aspect of *Our Town*. At the same time, the phrase *in part* lets readers know that this is not the only acclaimed element.)

SPECIFIC: Besides its lack of stage props, *Our Town*'s bittersweet portrayal of middle-class America has earned critical acclaim.

(This topic sentence begins a new paragraph that is linked to the previous paragraph by the transition *Besides its lack of stage props.* Now, each paragraph can focus on one main idea while remaining linked in theme.)

BROAD: *Teahouse of the August Moon* is a lighthearted satire of America's efforts to spread democratic ideals abroad.

(Explaining the satire, the efforts, the democratic ideals, and the results of the efforts would require many paragraphs of examples and reasons. In fact, this sentence could serve as the thesis for a composition. To work as a topic sentence, however, it must focus on *one* idea that can be fully developed in one paragraph.)

SPECIFIC: *Teahouse of the August Moon* portrays American capitalism as seen through the eyes of the Okinawans.

(This sentence focuses on one main idea: American capitalism as seen through the eyes of the Okinawans. Sentences explaining what the Okinawans see and what they think would develop the idea.)

BROAD: Vern Sneider, a novelist, wrote *Teahouse of the August Moon,* and John Patrick, an American playwright, wrote the Pulitzer Prize–winning screenplay of the same name.

(This sentence introduces at least two main ideas: Vern Sneider and John Patrick. In addition, readers may wonder if the novel and the screenplay are also main ideas.)

SPECIFIC: *Teahouse of the August Moon,* a novel by Vern Sneider, inspired John Patrick's Pulitzer Prize–winning screenplay of the same name.

(Even though this sentence mentions both writers and both literary works, the focus is different. Now, the main idea is the novel's inspiration of the screenplay. Note that an effective, focused topic sentence is rarely a compound sentence.)

Occasionally, a topic sentence is developed in two closely connected paragraphs. However, here we focus on one paragraph so that we can practice narrowing the topic to a tightly focused main idea.

ACTIVITY 2

On the lines provided, rewrite each broad topic sentence to be specific. More than one revision may be possible; focus your new topic sentence on the main idea you think is best.

> **Sample:**
>
> A successful playwright must know not only how to reveal a character's strengths and weaknesses but also how to make the audience care about him or her.
>
> _A successful playwright uses a character's weaknesses to awaken the_
>
> _audience's interest._
>
> **Alternate revision:**
>
> _A successful playwright knows how to reveal a character's weaknesses._

1. Master American dramatists include Neil Simon, Tennessee Williams, and Arthur Miller, all of whom have written plays included in school reading lists.

   _____

   _____

2. In Simon's _The Odd Couple,_ which has been produced as a Broadway play, a movie, and a television series, two friends decide to become apartment roommates, but their lifestyles clash—hilariously.

   _____

   _____

3. Williams's _The Glass Menagerie_ is a play about regret, hope, anger, and despair.

   _____

   _____

4. _A Streetcar Named Desire,_ a three-act play by Tennessee Williams, shows the mental and moral breakdown of a former Southern belle, Blanche Dubois.

   _____

   _____

5. In _Death of a Salesman,_ Miller's exploration of Willy Loman's personal and professional failures ends in Loman's tragic death.

   _____

   _____

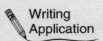
Writing a Focused Topic Sentence

If you were to write a short play about an event that has happened in your life, which event would you choose? Why would it make a good subject for a play? On a separate sheet of paper, make a list of events in your life, big or small, that might seem interesting to other people. Circle the one that could best be developed into a play.

Next, compose a topic sentence stating why a play about this event would attract an audience. Focus your statement on one defining quality of the event—the suspense of solving a theft, for example, or the realization of one of life's basic truths. Revise your topic sentence to make sure it is neither vague nor broad in scope.

Finally, write a paragraph developing your topic sentence with examples or reasons. If you realize that the paragraph is much too long (say, more than nine or ten sentences), revise your topic sentence again to make it more specific. Then edit the paragraph to support the revised topic sentence.

3. The topic sentence does not fit with the subject matter in the body of the paragraph.

Suppose the topic sentence in a paragraph is well written, but the supporting sentences support an idea *not* expressed by the topic sentence. Here is an example.

Tennessee Williams won prestigious awards for his most acclaimed screenplays. *Cat on a Hot Tin Roof* was produced in 1955. In the play, Big Daddy, the wealthy family patriarch, will soon celebrate his sixty-fifth birthday. The family mood is far from festive, however. One son, Brick, struggles with alcoholism and cannot accept the love his wife offers. The other son, Gooper, wants to take over Big Daddy's estate. The drama's success led to the 1958 film, starring Paul Newman and Elizabeth Taylor, based on the play.

In this example, the topic sentence promises a paragraph about Williams's awards. However, the supporting sentences give details about *Cat on a Hot Tin Roof*.

In this case, should you rewrite the topic sentence to fit the supporting sentences, or should you rewrite the supporting sentences to fit the topic sentence? To decide, ask yourself these questions:

(a) Do the supporting sentences develop a main idea that meets my writing purpose?

For example, if you are answering a test question, do the supporting sentences provide the best answer to this question? If the paragraph is part of a composition, do the sentences develop a main idea that supports the composition's thesis?

If the answer is yes, then rewrite the topic sentence to express the idea that the supporting sentences develop.

Williams's play *Cat on a Hot Tin Roof,* first produced in 1955, exposes the emotional turmoil within a family. In the play, Big Daddy, the wealthy family patriarch, will soon celebrate his sixty-fifth birthday. The family mood is far from festive, however. One son, Brick, struggles with alcoholism and cannot accept the love his wife offers. The other son, Gooper, wants to take over Big Daddy's estate. The drama's success led to the 1958 film, starring Paul Newman and Elizabeth Taylor, based on the play.

On the other hand, if the answer to the question in (a) is no, then go to (b), below.

(b) Does the topic sentence meet my writing purpose, but the supporting sentences go off topic?

In this case, do not change the topic sentence. Instead, rewrite the supporting sentences, making sure each one helps explain or prove the topic sentence.

Tennessee Williams won prestigious awards for his most acclaimed screenplays. Early in his career, in 1939, he received a Group Theatre award for *American Blues,* a group of one-act plays. In 1948, *A Streetcar Named Desire* earned Williams his first Pulitzer Prize. Seven years later, *Cat on a Hot Tin Roof* earned him another Pulitzer. Four of the playwright's works earned the New York Drama Critics' Circle Award.

This paragraph develops the topic sentence with examples of Williams's plays and the awards they earned. As you can see, *Cat on a Hot Tin Roof* is the subject of one sentence, but it is not the focus of the entire paragraph, as in the example above in (a).

ACTIVITY 3

Some of the following paragraphs have topic sentences that accurately state the paragraph's main idea. Others do not. First, underline the topic sentence. Then, on the blank before each paragraph, write *correct* if the topic sentences fits with the supporting sentences. Write *incorrect* if the topic sentence does not fit with the supporting sentences.

> **Samples:**
>
> _correct_ **a.** The Globe Theatre was a famous London theater. Built by Richard and Cuthbert Burbage, the Globe was where Shakespeare performed his plays after 1599. The theater burned down in 1613 but was rebuilt the following year. Eventually, in 1644, the theater was pulled down for good.
>
> _incorrect_ **b.** A play is made up mostly of dialogue spoken among characters. The largest section of a play is the act, and a play may have one or more acts. For example, Shakespeare used a five-act structure in *Henry VIII,* while Tennessee Williams wrote *The Glass Menagerie* in one act. Within each act are scenes. Each scene consists of action that occurs in one stage setting. When the set is changed, a new scene begins.

_____ 1. Basic stage terminology tells an actor where to stand onstage. For example, the part of the stage nearest the audience is called downstage. The part farthest away from the audience is upstage. Of course, the area between these areas is simply center stage. Each of these parts of the stage can be designated left, right, or center. Directions are determined from the actor's point of view as he or she faces the audience.

_____ 2. A playwright uses dramatic devices to compose a play that is both interesting and creative. A character delivering a soliloquy speaks to himself, or perhaps to the world in general. At the time, no other characters are in the scene. The purpose of this dramatic device is to reveal the speaker's thoughts to the audience without revealing them to another character in the play.

_____ 3. The Pulitzer Prize for Drama is a major literary award. It is given to playwrights of outstanding American plays. For example, Tennessee Williams has garnered the prize twice for plays about Southern families. Typically the Pulitzer is given yearly, although in some years no playwright has earned the award. To find the winner, a drama jury attends plays in New York and in regional theaters.

_____ 4. In the acting business, good looks may get you an audition, but acting skill gets you the job. Makeup includes traditional face makeup, of course. But it also encompasses other techniques of altering or enhancing actors' appearances. Wigs are a good example. So is hair coloring, both real and "fake" (such as baby powder dusted on to create the look of graying hair). Makeup may also include false noses or ears or even teeth. More elaborate makeup may include body paint, glitter, or other applications.

_____ 5. At the end of a scene, actors usually exit upstage. When used as a noun, _upstage_ refers to the area of a stage that is farthest away from the audience. As a verb, _upstage_ means "to take the audience's attention away from another performer." To upstage someone, an actor moves upstage. As a result, the other actor turns his or her back on the audience to face the actor.

Rewrite two of the topic sentences in Activity 3 that do not fit with their supporting sentences. On the lines below, identify the item number of the topic sentence (1, 2, 3, 4, or 5 from Activity 3), then write your revised topic sentence.

Sample:

_____ *b* _____ A written play is divided into distinct sections.

_____ 1. _____

_____

_____ 2. _____

_____

Writing
Application
Revising the Topic Sentence

Who is one of your favorite actors? Why is he or she a favorite with you? To develop your ideas, brainstorm details on a separate sheet of paper.

Next, write a paragraph of about **six to eight** sentences explaining your answers to the above questions. Make sure your topic sentence accurately states the main idea of the paragraph.

With your teacher's approval, exchange paragraphs with a classmate. Carefully read the paragraph you receive and underline the topic sentence. Does the topic sentence accurately state the main idea developed by the supporting sentences? Or does the topic sentence promise one main idea, but the supporting sentences discuss something else? Write a note explaining your opinion to your classmate; be as specific as possible in your explanation. Share the results with your classmate.

If your classmate thought your topic sentence was off target, examine the paragraph again. Then, if you agree with your classmate, rewrite the topic sentence to make it specific to the supporting sentences.

Writing
Application
Revising the Topic Sentence in a Previously Written Paragraph

In Lesson 12, you practiced writing strong clincher sentences for various paragraphs. In the Writing Application on page 118, you wrote a paragraph telling why you do or do not enjoy reading poetry. Find the paragraph you wrote and read it again. In particular, study the topic sentence. In what way or ways could you make it stronger?

Using the checklist on page 162, revise the topic sentence for the paragraph. Then write a fresh copy of the paragraph with its new topic sentence and underline the topic sentence.

Revising for Unity

As you learned in Lesson 11, all sentences in a paragraph should support or develop the main idea stated in the topic sentence. Not only that, but sentences should flow logically from one to the next, aided by transitional words and phrases when appropriate. When all sentences focus tightly on one idea and clearly link together, the paragraph has unity.

Compare the following examples.

EXAMPLE 1: LACK OF UNITY

1Do you love chocolate chip cookies? **2**Do you wish they were more healthful? **3**Many people wish for snacks that won't wreck their healthy-eating plan. **4**You will flip for chocolate chip pancakes. **5**Pancakes are quick and easy to make. **6**These chocolate treats taste much like the traditional cookie. **7**Cookies are best eaten warm, with a glass of cold milk on the side. **8**Pancakes' fat and sugar content is much lower. **9**You can find nutrition information printed somewhere on the package. **10**Use any pancake mix. **11**Betty Crocker® and Arrowhead Mills® both make good mixes. **12**Prepare the mix. **13**Follow package directions. **14**Add a half teaspoon of vanilla extract and a half cup of mini–chocolate chips. **15**Cook according to package directions. **16**Eat warm or cooled. **17**Do not add syrup or butter. **18**Eat them like cookies.

This main idea of this paragraph is unclear because the sentences focus on several ideas, not one main idea. No transitions are present to help readers connect the different ideas.

S1, S6, S7, and S18 focus on or mention cookies.

S2, S3, S8, and S9 focus on or allude to health concerns.

S4–S6, S8, and S10–S18 focus on pancakes, although the point about pancakes varies among the sentences.

Because these sentences do not focus tightly on one main idea, and because there are no transitions to help readers see the connection among ideas, *the paragraph lacks unity.*

EXAMPLE 2: UNITY

1Do you love chocolate chip cookies but wish they were more healthful? **2**Then you will flip for chocolate chip pancakes. **3**These chocolate treats taste much like the traditional cookie, yet their fat and sugar content is much lower. **4**To make them, use any pancake mix. **5**Prepare the mix according to package directions, except add a half teaspoon of vanilla extract and a half cup of mini–chocolate chips to the batter. **6**Then cook according to package directions. **7**Eat warm or cooled, without syrup or butter, as you would cookies.

This paragraph focuses on one main idea.

S1 and S2 identify the main idea: chocolate chip pancakes as a healthy alternative to chocolate chip cookies. The transitional word *Then* links S1 and S2, showing a cause-effect relationship.

S3 states why readers will want to try the pancakes.

S4–S6 identify the steps in making the pancakes. The steps are in sequential order, with transitions (*To make them, except,* and *Then*) to link ideas.

S7 gives closure by stating how best to eat the treat. It drives home the main idea by implying a comparison of the pancakes and cookies.

Because all sentences relate to one main idea, because transitions help readers see relationships between ideas, and because the information is given in a logical, sequential order, *this paragraph has unity.*

When you revise your paragraphs to create unity, use the following checklist.

Revising for Unity

Revise each paragraph to correct the following errors:

_____ sentences off topic

_____ more than one main idea

_____ unclear transitions

_____ unclear or illogical relationships between ideas (*Note:* A table of transitional words and phrases is on page 109.)

ACTIVITY 1 _____

Using the "Revising for Unity" checklist above, revise the following paragraph. Write your revised paragraph on a separate sheet of paper.

My best friend has one abhorrent quality. He is habitually late. No matter what the occasion, he arrives late. He and I coach a neighborhood T-ball team. I really love baseball. Coaching T-ball is a way for me to help young kids discover their love of playing ball. Every Saturday morning I arrive on time. On some days, events at home make it difficult for me to be on time, such as the time my sister hogged the shower for twenty minutes. Thirty minutes go by (after I arrive). He waltzes in. He doesn't apologize. He was late meeting me for a movie. We missed the first thirty minutes. I told him how angry his lateness makes me. When you tell a friend about a fault, you should do so as tactfully as possible. He was surprised. Being late caused difficulty to others. It had never crossed his mind.

ACTIVITY 2

Using the "Revising for Unity" checklist on page 172, revise the following paragraph. Write your revised paragraph on a separate sheet of paper.

Voting is not as simple as checking a box. Deciding whom or what to vote for can be difficult. Examples of elections include those for class president, student council member, club leader, and student union president. There are several reasons. Take the presidential election. Are you planning to vote in the next election? For months before election day, competing parties barrage potential voters with propaganda. Speeches and advertisements build up strengths of one candidate. They denigrate the abilities of opponents. People become confused. They are uncertain what to believe. They try to see past the mudslinging. They ask themselves questions. What is really true? What is distorted fact or outright lie? Voting is a great way to help direct the course of history.

ACTIVITY 3

Using the "Revising for Unity" checklist on page 172, revise the following paragraph for unity. Write your revised paragraph on a separate sheet of paper.

My best friend gave me a gift for my birthday. It was a handmade certificate. It was for a mix CD. She would make it herself. The next weekend came. I took my certificate over to her house. I also took twenty of my favorite CDs. She made notes about which songs were my favorite. She copied each of these songs onto her computer. She burned each song onto a new, blank CD. I had one CD with twenty-five songs I love on it. What a great birthday gift! Making inexpensive birthday gifts does not have to seem "cheap" to the recipient.

 Writing Application

Revising a Paragraph for Unity

Write a paragraph using one of the topic sentences listed below, or write your own topic sentence. Then use the checklist on page 184 to revise the paragraph for unity. Use a separate sheet of paper for writing and revising the paragraph.

Choices for Topic Sentence

1. Music fans should keep their eyes on _____, a new artist.
2. Red meat is (*or* is not) the base for a healthful meal.
3. The best movie in theaters recently is _____.
4. _____ is a fun hobby for several reasons.
5. My worst pet peeve is _____.

Writing Application

Revising A Classmate's
Paragraph for Unity

Write a paragraph beginning with one of the topic sentences listed below, or write your own topic sentence. Include at least **six** sentences in your paragraph, and write on a separate sheet of paper.

Choices for Topic Sentence

1. My most indispensable possession is _____.

2. Asking someone out on a date does not have to be difficult.

3. Gossip is (*or* is not) harmless fun.

4. Beauty is in the eye of the beholder.

5. Balancing school and a job is (*or* is not) beneficial to the student.

With your teacher's approval, exchange paragraphs with a classmate. Use the checklist on page 184 to revise your classmate's paragraph for unity. Write your revision below the original paragraph. Then share the results with your classmate.

Writing Application

Revising a Previously Written
Paragraph for Unity

Gather several compositions or pieces of writing you have done in school, such as reports, essays, tests, or homework that required written paragraphs.

Scan the pieces you collected, looking for a paragraph that lacks unity.

On a separate sheet of paper, copy the paragraph as it is. As you copy it, think about which qualities are robbing the paragraph of unity.

Using the checklist on page 184 revise the paragraph for unity, writing the revision below the original. Once you are finished, think about how your grade on the original assignment might have been different if this and all paragraphs for the assignment were unified.

Revising the Order of Sentences

In Lessons 13 and 14, you learned that the order of sentences in a paragraph can strengthen—or weaken—the paragraph. Compare the following paragraphs.

EXAMPLE 1: REASONS ARE JUMBLED IN NO PARTICULAR ORDER

[1]Tanned skin may look healthy, but in reality it is damaged. [2]The tan results from the sun's ultraviolet rays hitting the skin. [3]Consequently, skin that is frequently tanned eventually becomes wrinkly and tough, like leather. [4]In some cases, sun damage leads to skin cancer, whether the skin is leathery or not. [5]Even if skin does not burn before tanning, it is nevertheless harmed. [6]Besides making skin produce pigment (the "tan"), these rays make skin less supple. [7]For fair-skinned people, a tan usually begins with a sunburn. [8]The burn can cause blisters to form on the skin; damaged skin dies and peels off.

This paragraph has a strong topic sentence (S1), but the supporting reasons are jumbled, as though the writer wrote them—and left them—in whatever order they occurred to him. Here are the reasons and their relative levels of importance:

Skin becomes wrinkly and tough (S2 and S3; one of the strongest reasons).

Skin cancer develops (S4; the strongest reason).

Skin loses suppleness (S5 and S6; a reason slightly less powerful than that in S2 and S3).

Skin burns, blisters, and peels (S7 and S8; least strong because it deals with a one-time sunburn rather than lasting effects).

The paragraph ends on its weakest note, leaving a mediocre impression on readers.

EXAMPLE 2: REASONS ARE ARRANGED FROM LEAST TO MOST POWERFUL

[1]Tanned skin may look healthy, but in reality it is damaged. [2]For fair-skinned people, a tan usually begins with a sunburn. [3]The burn can cause blisters to form on the skin; damaged skin dies and peels off. [4]Even if skin does not burn before tanning, it is nevertheless harmed. [5]The tan results from the sun's ultraviolet rays hitting the skin. [6]Besides making skin produce pigment (the "tan"), these rays make skin less supple. [7]Consequently, skin that is frequently tanned eventually becomes wrinkly and tough, like leather. [8]In some cases, sun damage leads to skin cancer, whether the skin is leathery or not.

In this revised version of the paragraph, the supporting reasons build from least to most powerful.

Skin burns, blisters, and peels (S2 and S3; short-term effects).

S4 works as a transition from sunburns to tans.

Skin loses suppleness (S5 and S6; a more lasting effect).

Skin becomes wrinkly and tough (S7; a long-term effect and more unappealing than loss of suppleness).

Skin cancer develops (S8; the most dangerous effect and therefore the most powerful reason).

The paragraph packs a punch because it ends on its strongest note. While readers may shrug off a one-time sunburn, they are unlikely to shrug off leathery skin.

QUESTION: How can I revise my paragraphs to create the most effective arrangement of examples or reasons?

ANSWER: Use the checklist below to arrange or revise the order of supporting sentences.

Arranging the Order of Sentences

Revise the order of sentences in a paragraph by

_____ arranging reasons to build up to the strongest

_____ arranging examples to build up to the most important

_____ arranging examples related to a time sequence in chronological order

_____ arranging examples of steps in a process in order from first to last

_____ in comparisons, arranging like qualities together and unlike qualities together

ACTIVITY 1 _____

Using the "Arranging the Order of Sentences" checklist above, revise the following paragraph. Write your revised paragraph on a separate sheet of paper. Then, on the same page underneath the paragraph, write an explanation of why you arranged the examples in the order you chose.

Cleaning the bathroom on Saturday morning can be dangerous to your health. Why? Some ingredients in household cleaners are health hazards. Lye (sodium hydroxide), found in toilet bowl cleaners and tub/tile cleaners, can cause blindness if splashed in the eyes. Hydrochloric and phosphoric acids, found in cleaners for toilets and tubs and in lime removers, emit vapors that irritate the eyes, nose, and throat. Wheezing and sneezing may result. Butyl cellosolve, an ingredient in window cleaners, is easily absorbed through the skin and into the bloodstream. It damages the liver and central nervous system. It can destroy kidneys.

Using the "Arranging the Order of Sentences" checklist on page 176, revise the following paragraph. Write your revised paragraph on a separate sheet of paper. Then, on the same page underneath the paragraph, write an explanation of why you arranged the examples in the order you chose.

Nontoxic alternatives to toxic household cleaners exist. For more cleaning power, mix three parts baking soda with one part liquid soap (*not* liquid detergent). You can mix up enough to last a month, but be sure to keep the container tightly sealed. Add a few drops of your favorite essential oil for a nice scent. A simple, convenient cleaner is a paste formed of baking soda and water. Simply mix it as you need it and rinse the surface well to avoid a powdery residue. With a little elbow grease, this basic cleanser scours all surfaces without scratching, without fumes, and without health hazards. Either of these cleaners not only keeps your home clean but also keeps your home safe.

 Writing Application

Revising the Order of Sentences

Have you ever noticed a friend doing something that she or he thought was impressive, but in actuality the act was harmful? Maintaining a deep tan all summer long is one example. The tan may look impressive, but it could lead to skin cancer.

On a separate sheet of paper, brainstorm a list of activities that some people think are impressive but that are actually harmful. Besides tanning, a few ideas to get you started are smoking, speeding, and riding a bicycle without a helmet.

From your prewriting, choose one behavior and write a paragraph telling how the seemingly impressive behavior is actually harmful. Revise the paragraph to arrange the reasons in order from least to most powerful.

On the same page, beneath the paragraph, write an explanation of why you arranged the reasons in the order that you did.

 **Writing Application**

Revising the Order of Someone Else's Sentences

What is one daring activity that you would like to experience or accomplish? Perhaps it is physically daring, such as skydiving, rock climbing, or body surfing. Perhaps it is intellectually or emotionally daring, such as becoming president, becoming a heart surgeon, or singing onstage in front of thousands of people.

On a separate sheet of paper, brainstorm a list of daring experiences that interest you. Then choose one to write about. Write a paragraph giving reasons why you want to have this daring experience. Give the reasons in whatever order they occur to you.

With your teacher's approval, exchange papers with a classmate. Read the paragraph you receive, evaluating the arrangement of sentences. What do you think the most effective arrangement would be?

On the same sheet of paper, below the paragraph, write a revision in which you arrange the sentences in the best possible order. Underneath that, explain why you chose the order that you did. Share the results with your classmate.

Revising Sentence Order in Previously Written Paragraphs

In Lesson 9, you wrote several paragraphs. At that point in your study, your focus was making sure all sentences in a paragraph told about one main idea. Now, however, you are aware that all sentences must not only relate to one main idea, but they also must develop the idea by giving details in the most effective order.

Find the paragraphs you wrote for the Writing Application on page 103. On a new sheet of paper, revise the paragraphs using the "Arranging the Order of Sentences" checklist given earlier in this lesson.

20 Adding Sentence Variety

In Lessons 1 and 3, you studied the four sentence types and how to write sentences that vary in length and structure. At that point in your study, you focused on individual sentences and how to make each one concise, clear, and a pleasure to read. Now, you can use those sentence-writing skills to create strong, effective paragraphs. How? By varying the type, length, and structure of sentences within the paragraph. Compare the following examples:

EXAMPLE 1: MONOTONOUS DUE TO REPETITIVE SENTENCE STRUCTURE

Americans are fond of ethnic foods. They often go to Chinese restaurants. They order moo goo gai pan or shrimp lo mein. They visit a bakery. They are quite likely to buy Danish pastry, French éclairs, or Jewish rye bread. They enjoy corned beef and cabbage on St. Patrick's Day. They enjoy it at other times too. They are not necessarily Irish. They are especially fond of Italian foods. They eat spaghetti and meatballs, macaroni and cheese, and pizza.

In this paragraph, every sentence is a simple sentence (one subject and one verb). Because all the sentences follow the same pattern of subject-verb-object, they sound alike. The repetitive structure is monotonous. Not only that, but the sentences are all approximately the same length, adding to the monotony. Overall, nothing about the structure of the sentences grabs readers, keeps them interested, or makes the sentences—and thus the paragraph—a pleasure to read.

EXAMPLE 2: APPEALING DUE TO VARIED SENTENCE STRUCTURE

[1]Americans are fond of ethnic foods. [2]Often, they go to Chinese restaurants for moo goo gai pan or shrimp lo mein. [3]When they visit a bakery, they are quite likely to buy Danish pastry, French éclairs, or Jewish rye bread. [4]On St. Patrick's Day and at other times, they enjoy corned beef and cabbage even though they may not be Irish. [5]In particular, they are fond of Italian foods. [6]What American has not had spaghetti and meatballs, macaroni and cheese, or pizza?

This paragraph is a pleasure to read because it has a variety in sentences types, lengths, structures, and purposes.

S3 and S4 are complex sentences, while the others are simple.

S1 is quite short, while S2, S5, and S6 are longer. Longer still are S3 and S4.

Only one sentence (S1) begins with the subject. Others begin with an adverb (S2), an adverb clause (S3), and prepositional phrases (S4).

S6 adds variety by taking the form of a question.

QUESTION: How can I make sure my paragraph has sentence variety?

ANSWER: First of all, don't worry about adding sentence variety when you write the first draft of a paragraph. Your first goal is to get your ideas on paper and to arrange the examples or reasons in the paragraph in the most effective order. Then, using the checklist below, revise the paragraph to add sentence variety.

Adding Sentence Variety

Add sentence variety in a paragraph by

_____ varying sentence types (simple, compound, complex, compound-complex)

_____ varying sentence lengths

_____ including an occasional question, exclamation, or command/polite request, when appropriate

_____ varying sentence beginnings

_____ using appositives

_____ using verbals (participles, infinitives, gerunds)

EXAMPLES:	Moo goo gai pan, *a Chinese dish*, is a flavorful mixture of mushrooms and chicken.
	A flavorful Chinese dish, moo goo gai pan is a mixture of mushrooms and chicken.
EXAMPLE:	*Visiting a bakery*, we bought Danish pastry and French éclairs.
	(The participle is *Visiting*, and *Visiting a bakery* is a participial phrase.)
EXAMPLES:	*To celebrate*, we ate corned beef and cabbage.
	We ate corned beef and cabbage *to celebrate St. Patrick's Day*.
	(This sentence has an infinitive phrase.)
EXAMPLE:	*Ordering a pizza for delivery* is a Friday night treat.
	(The gerund is *Ordering*, and *Ordering a pizza for delivery* is a gerund phrase.)

KEY TERMS

An *appositive* is a word or word group that identifies or renames a noun or pronoun.

A *verbal* is a verb form that is used not as a verb but rather as a noun, an adjective, or an adverb. Participles, infinitives, and gerunds are kinds of verbals.

A *participle* is a verb form that may be used as part of a verb phrase or as an adjective.

An *infinitive* is a verb form that can be used as a noun, an adjective, or an adverb. Most infinitives begin with *to*, as in *to eat*.

A *gerund* is a verb form used as a noun in a sentence. A gerund ends in *ing*.

ACTIVITY 1

Using the "Adding Sentence Variety" checklist above, revise the following paragraph. Write your revised paragraph on a separate sheet of paper.

The Stonehenge Mall food court offers American and ethnic foods. The foods are tasty. Some people are hamburger fans. Burger House serves up cheeseburgers, barbecue burgers, and veggie burgers. Some people prefer something spicier. They can create their own combination platter at Hungry Wok. They can choose from orange chicken, beef with broccoli, crab puffs, lo mein noodles, and more. Some people crave Italian. They can go to Pie in the Sky. They can order pizza by the slice. They can also get lasagna, spaghetti and meatballs, and ziti with marinara sauce. There are other fabulous eateries. Visit the food court today. Bring a hungry stomach.

Using the "Adding Sentence Variety" checklist on page 180, revise the following paragraph. Write your revised paragraph on a separate sheet of paper.

The tortilla is a staple of Mexican food. It is flat and circular. It may be made of flour or corn. Breakfast tacos use tortillas. A warm flour tortilla is folded in half. Scrambled eggs and piping hot chorizo (sausage) fill it. There is lunch. Corn tortillas may be fried briefly in oil. They are crispy. They may be flat or folded. The flat ones are layered with refried beans, ground beef, cheese, and diced tomatoes. This is a tostada. The folded ones become tacos. They are filled with ground beef or chicken, cheese, lettuce, and tomato. There are other tortilla dishes. They include tortilla soup (chicken broth, chicken pieces, and crunchy corn tortilla strips). They also include quesadillas (a grilled cheese sandwich made with a folded flour tortilla).

Writing Application

Adding Sentence Variety

What is your favorite kind of ethnic food? Examples mentioned in the lesson so far include Chinese, Danish, French, Jewish, Irish, Italian, and Mexican. Others include Thai, Japanese, Mediterranean, African, German, and Jamaican, to name a few.

Write a paragraph telling why you like a particular kind of ethnic food. Once you get your ideas down on paper and arrange the sentences in an effective order, revise the paragraph for sentence variety. Use the checklist on page 180.

Writing Application

Revising Previously Written Paragraphs to Add Sentence Variety

In Lesson 13, you wrote paragraphs developed with examples. At that point in your study, your focus was making sure that the examples supported the main idea and were arranged in an effective order. Now, in addition, you know that sentence variety can make a paragraph even stronger.

Find the paragraph you wrote for either Activity 2 (pages 122–123) or the Writing Application on page 126. Make a copy of the paragraph, either by hand or using a photocopying machine. Keep the original for yourself.

Next, with your teacher's approval, exchange paragraphs with a classmate. You have two tasks: (1) revise your classmate's paragraph for sentence variety, and (2) revise your own paragraph for sentence variety. Use the revision checklist on page 180.

Finally, compare both of your revisions with the two revisions your classmate wrote. Talk about which parts of each paragraph are especially strong. Discuss whether one revision seems more powerful than the other, and why.

Writing Application

Revising Previously Written Paragraphs to Add Sentence Variety

This writing application is much like the one on page 181, only this time you will use a paragraph you wrote for Lesson 14, "Developing a Paragraph With Reasons." Find the paragraph you wrote for either Activity 3 (pages 131–132) or the Writing Application on page 132. Make a copy of the paragraph, either by hand or using a photocopying machine. Keep the original for yourself.

Next, with your teacher's approval, exchange paragraphs with a classmate. You have two tasks: (1) revise your classmate's paragraph for sentence variety, and (2) revise your own paragraph for sentence variety. Use the revision checklist on page 180.

Finally, compare both of your revisions with the two revisions your classmate wrote. Talk about which parts of each paragraph are especially strong. Discuss whether one revision seems more powerful than the other, and why.

21 Review of Paragraph Revision

Recall this checklist for revising the topic sentence in a paragraph:

Revise topic sentences to make sure they are

_____ specific, not vague

_____ focused, not broad

_____ in agreement with supporting sentences, not off topic

ACTIVITY 1

On the lines provided, rewrite each topic sentence to correct its weakness. Use your own knowledge and imagination to provide the specifics necessary to the revision.

> **Samples:**
>
> **a.** Any business can create a profitable demand for its product.
>
> *Any business can use advertising to create a profitable demand for its product.*
>
> **b.** Follow these procedures to set up a new customer account and to track inventory.
>
> *Follow these procedures to set up a new customer account.*

1. Good business sense is essential to success.

_____

_____

2. Prices affect sales.

_____

_____

3. Important aspects of a business are overhead, products or services, and customers.

_____

_____

4. A business plan must be strong.

_____

_____

5. Print, radio, and television advertising have different sets of requirements.

_____

_____

Read the following paragraph. Then choose the sentence (A, B, or C) that would make the best topic sentence for the paragraph. Finally, explain why your choice is a good one (use the revision checklist above to analyze and explain strengths).

For example, the floor space a retail store occupies requires a lease or mortgage payment each month. This cost is figured into overhead. Of course, basic floor space is not enough. Utilities such as electricity to light the store and run cash registers or computers are another part of overhead. Even more important than rent and utilities is payroll, for no business can survive without labor. Business owners must not only pay wages but must also pay taxes and, perhaps, health plan premiums. All these costs and more can create a substantial overhead.

Choices:

A. Many business owners take out a loan to cover the start-up costs of a new business.

B. A successful business owner must be able to balance the monthly budget.

C. In business terminology, *overhead* is all the operating expenses of a company.

BEST TOPIC SENTENCE: _____

WHY IT IS BEST: _____

_____

_____

Recall this checklist for revising a paragraph for unity:

Revise paragraphs to correct the following errors:

_____ sentences off topic

_____ more than one main idea

_____ unclear transitions

_____ unclear or illogical relationships between ideas

Using the checklist above, revise the following paragraph for unity. Write your revised paragraph on a separate sheet of paper.

Successful businesspeople share certain key traits. Ambition drives them to work hard. They work hard to accomplish goals. A good way to keep track of goals is to use a calendar or day planner system. They have detailed knowledge of their company's product or service. Products include anything tangible, such as auto parts, shampoo, shoes, and tires.

It helps them. They perform their jobs. They reach their goals. They have persistence. They do not give up. They are faced with long hours, tough competition, and a boss's demands. Some bosses are better than others in getting employees to do their best. There is ambition, knowledge, and persistence. They define the ideal businessperson.

Writing Application — Revising a Paragraph for Unity

Select one of the topic sentences you wrote in Activity 1 and use it to write a complete paragraph of at least **seven** sentences. (Use a separate sheet of paper.) Then, underneath this first draft of the paragraph, revise the paragraph to make it stronger. To guide your revision, use the checklist for revising a paragraph for unity. Finally, underneath the revision, write an explanation of why your paragraph has unity.

Recall this checklist for revising the order of sentences in a paragraph:

Revise the order of sentences in a paragraph by

_____ arranging reasons to build up to the strongest

_____ arranging examples to build up to the most important

_____ arranging examples related to a time sequence in chronological order

_____ arranging examples of steps in a process in order from first to last

_____ in comparisons, arranging like qualities together and unlike qualities together

ACTIVITY 4

Using the checklist above, revise the following paragraph to achieve the most effective order of sentences. Write your revised paragraph on a separate sheet of paper. Then, on the same page underneath the paragraph, write an explanation of why you arranged the reasons in the order you chose.

In business, competition for customers can be fierce. A huge chain bookstore may drive "mom and pop" bookstores completely out of business by buying in bulk and setting discount prices. One coffee shop may temporarily steal its rival's customers by mailing out money-saving coupons. A clothing store may build a bigger customer base than its rival by staying open longer hours. Evidently, in business, competition is the name of the game.

Revising the Order of Sentences in a Classmate's Paragraph

Select one of the topic sentences you wrote in Activity 1 and use it to write a complete paragraph of at least **seven** sentences. Write the sentences in the order in which they occur to you. (Use a separate sheet of paper.)

Then, with your teacher's approval, exchange paragraphs with a classmate. Read the paragraph you receive, evaluating the order of sentences. What do you think the most effective arrangement would be?

On the same sheet of paper, below the paragraph, write a revision in which you arrange the sentences in the best possible order. To guide your revision, use the checklist for arranging the order of sentences. Underneath that, explain why you chose the order that you did. Share the results with your classmate.

Recall this checklist for adding sentence variety to a paragraph:

Add sentence variety in a paragraph by

_____ varying sentence types (simple, compound, complex, compound-complex)

_____ varying sentence lengths

_____ including an occasional question, exclamation, or command/polite request, when appropriate

_____ varying sentence beginnings

_____ using appositives

_____ using verbals (participles, infinitives, gerunds)

ACTIVITY 5 _____

Using the checklist above, revise the following paragraph. Write your revised paragraph on a separate sheet of paper.

A common way to start a business is with a franchise. The businessperson buys the franchise. Examples of franchises include fast-food restaurants, photocopy stores, and retail stores. A businessperson pays the *franchiser*. The franchiser is the company owning rights to the business. The businessperson pays for rights. Rights include usage of logos, recipes, copyrights, trade secrets, and other assets. The terms of the arrangement may also require more. The franchisee may pay a portion of profits or a flat fee. This payment is usually monthly. The business owner buys these things from a franchiser. He or she can immediately turn his or her attention to other things. He or she can run the business. He or she can make it profitable.

Adding Sentence Variety

Choose a paragraph you wrote for one of the Writing Applications earlier in this lesson (pages 185 and 186). On a separate sheet of paper, revise that paragraph to add sentence variety. To guide your work, use the checklist for adding sentence variety. Finally, underneath the revision, explain at least two techniques you used. (For example, *I used the adverb clause <u>While scientists worked</u> to begin the third sentence, which adds variety in sentence beginnings.*)

Paragraph Revision Checklist

Use this checklist as a guide when you write and revise paragraphs. It includes the characteristics of strong paragraphs (taught in Lessons 9–16) and techniques for revising paragraphs to make them stronger (taught in Lessons 17–21).

WRITING PARAGRAPHS

Make sure paragraphs are strong and unified by including these qualities:

All Paragraphs:

_____ appropriate length

_____ unity

_____ topic sentence (in body paragraphs)

_____ well-developed reasons or examples that support the topic sentence, arranged in a logical sequence

_____ clincher sentence, if appropriate

Introductory Paragraph:

_____ identification of the composition's topic

_____ narrowing of the topic to one specific idea

_____ expression of the main idea in a thesis

Conclusion Paragraph:

_____ restatement of the thesis

_____ summary of key ideas

_____ final emphasis on value of composition's content

REVISING THE TOPIC SENTENCE

Revise topic sentences to make sure they are

_____ specific, not vague

_____ focused, not broad

_____ in agreement with supporting sentences, not off topic

REVISING FOR UNITY

Revise paragraphs to correct the following errors:

_____ sentences off topic

_____ more than one main idea

_____ unclear transitions

_____ unclear or illogical relationships between ideas

ARRANGING THE ORDER OF SENTENCES

Revise the order of sentences in a paragraph by

_____ arranging reasons to build up to the strongest

_____ arranging examples to build up to the most important

_____ arranging examples related to a time sequence in chronological order

_____ arranging examples of steps in a process in order from first to last

_____ in comparisons, arranging like qualities together and unlike qualities together

ADDING SENTENCE VARIETY

Add sentence variety in a paragraph by

_____ varying sentence types (simple, compound, complex, compound-complex)

_____ varying sentence lengths

_____ including an occasional question, exclamation, or command/polite request, when appropriate

_____ varying sentence beginnings

_____ using appositives

_____ using verbals (participles, infinitives, gerunds)

Paragraph Revision

The following research applications encourage you to take your **paragraph revision** beyond this workbook and into real life. Each assignment asks you to gather information on one of the themes in the previous lessons and to write and revise paragraphs about your findings. Enjoy your research and take pride in using your skills of paragraph revision!

THEME: Drama

SKILL: Revising the Topic Sentence

Choose a topic relating to drama that you would like to know more about. Here are a few ideas to get you started:

musical theater	women playwrights	set design
auditions	Broadway	the Tony Awards
a dramatic device (i.e., monologue)		

Choose one of the topics above, or another topic, and find out more about it. Starting with a search on the Internet can lead to helpful definitions, official Web sites, books, and articles.

Next, narrow down the information to an idea about which you can write **two** paragraphs. Finally, write your paragraphs. Edit each topic sentence to make sure it is specific and on target, *not* vague, broad, or off target.

THEME: Unity

SKILL: Revising for Unity

Unity is a concept that shows up in more places than you might think. For example, a musical artist may give his or her CD unity by including songs that develop a central theme. A television show has unity when all the action and dialogue ties together to develop one main plot. Political leaders throughout history have sought to unify—or break the unity of—tribes, colonies, states, countries, or other groups.

Choose one of the examples of unity above, or choose another that interests you. Do a little research to find out specific examples of or reasons for the unity you are investigating. Gather enough information to write two paragraphs about the topic. Then write the paragraphs. Finally, use the checklist on page 184 to revise your paragraphs for unity.

THEME: Safety and Health

SKILL: Revising the Order of Sentences

To ensure that workers are safe on the job, the U.S. Department of Labor formed the Occupational Safety and Health Administration, or OSHA (pronounced as one word, OSH-ah). This organization investigates all kinds of health and safety risks, from asphalt fumes to avian flu to carpal tunnel syndrome. It educates employers about hazards and educates workers about how to stay safe.

Find out more about a specific safety or health risk. Go to OSHA's Web site, at www.osha.gov, and click on the SAFETY/HEALTH TOPICS link in the lower right-hand column. For example, why are asphalt fumes a health risk? What is avian flu, and how might someone contract it? What is carpal tunnel syndrome, and what can a worker to do try to prevent it?

Write two paragraphs about your findings (include at least six sentences per paragraph). Then use the checklist on page 188 to arrange the sentences in the most effective order.

THEME: Food

SKILL: Adding Sentence Variety

Is there any such thing as "American food," or have American dishes simply developed from various ethnic origins? For example, macaroni and cheese seems classically American, but really the dish is Italian. And hot dogs? German immigrants introduced the sausage-in-a-bun idea. Biscuits? Perhaps they are British scones in disguise.

Choose a food or dish that most Americans would consider American and research its origins. Find out what culture originated the dish and when the food came to the United States. Look for basic details about the dish and any American alterations of the original version. The Internet will be a help to your research, as always, but don't overlook ethnic cookbooks.

Write two paragraphs telling about your findings. For example, the first paragraph could tell where or how the dish originated, and the second paragraph could tell why Americans claim it as their own. Finally, use the checklist on page 188 to revise your paragraphs for sentence variety.

THEME: Business

SKILL: Revising Paragraphs

What is one product or service you could offer as a one-person business? Babysitting and dog walking are classic endeavors, but you could be more creative. If you love to cook, cater meals instead of babysitting for busy families. If you love sports, offer one-on-one coaching sessions. If you are good at making household repairs, offer handyman services.

Choose one product or service and find out crucial information and steps to building a business around it. For example, how much should you charge? What equipment or supplies, if any, would you need? Would you need capital (money) to get started? How would you find and attract customers?

Use the information you gather to write two paragraphs telling about your business idea. For example, paragraph 1 could introduce and explain the basic idea, and paragraph 2 could outline the steps to starting up the business or could explain essential information such as prices, work hours, and so on.

Finally, use the checklist on pages 187–188 to revise your paragraphs, making them as strong and effective as possible.

Paragraph Revision

PART 1

Directions: The following passage is the first half of a draft of a composition. The sentences are numbered for ease of reference. Some parts of the passage need to be revised. Read the passage, then circle the letter of the best answer to each question below and write it on the blank.

Personal Space

[1]You have probably heard the expression, "You are invading my space." [2]Perhaps you yourself have said this to a nosy sibling or a curious parent. [3]Personal space can be anything from a school locker to a car, a bedroom, or the space around our own body. [4]Examples of spaces that are not personal are kitchens, classrooms, and bus stops. [5]Personal space—of whatever kind—is worth protecting; we rely on it for comfort and privacy.

[6]Inside our lockers we keep books and notebooks, of course, but we also keep personal items such as photos and love notes or a hairbrush and extra stick of deodorant. [7]Even if we have nothing to hide in our locker (that is, nothing that breaks school rules), we still insist that the contents remain private. [8]School officials, we believe, should not have the right to open our locker and poke around inside; that would be an invasion of privacy.

[9]We may be fortunate enough to own our own car. [10]We consider it a personal space. [11]We make rules that others must follow in order to ride in our car: no smoking, no eating, no dogs. [12]We control the radio dials or the CD player. [13]The fuzzy dice hanging from the rearview mirror are ours, as is the bobble-head doll in the rear window. [14]In short, this is space that we control in a way that maintains our own comfort. [15]Other aspects of car ownership, however, are not so comfortable, such as changing a tire or washing the car.

_____ 1. Which is the best revision of the underlined portion of sentence 5 (reproduced below)?

Personal space—of whatever kind—is worth <u>protecting; we rely</u> on it for comfort and privacy.

A. protecting; therefore, we rely

B. protecting, although we rely

C. protecting because we rely

D. protecting; second, we rely

_____ **2.** Which of the following revisions to sentence 9 is most needed?

    F. Move "to own our own car" to the beginning of sentence 9.

    G. Change sentence 9 to an adverb clause beginning with "If we are," and join sentence 9 to sentence 10.

    H. Delete "enough."

    J. Add "For example," to the beginning of sentence 9.

_____ **3.** Which of the following sentences would make the best topic sentence for the second paragraph, to be inserted just before sentence 6?

    A. School lockers are a small personal space, but their lockable privacy is priceless.

    B. School lockers are very important personal spaces.

    C. At school, we need a place to store books, photos, love notes, hairbrushes, and deodorant.

    D. Personal spaces such as school lockers are not the best place to store items that break school rules.

_____ **4.** Which sentence creates a lack of unity in its paragraph?

    F. sentence 11

    G. sentence 7

    H. sentence 15

    J. sentence 3

_____ **5.** Which is the best revision of the underlined portion of sentence 11 (reproduced below)?

<u>We make</u> rules that others must follow in order to ride in our car: no smoking, no eating, no dogs.

    A. Next, we make

    B. Similarly, we make

    C. Most important, we make

    D. For instance, we make

_____ **6.** Which sentence creates a lack of unity in its paragraph?

    F. sentence 1

    G. sentence 4

    H. sentence 8

    J. sentence 12

_____ **7.** To add sentence variety, which is the best revision of sentence 1?

    A. Has anyone ever said to you, "You are invading my space"?

    B. A common expression is, "You are invading my space."

    C. "You are invading my space" is a common expression.

    D. Most people have heard the expression, "You are invading my space."

Directions: The following passage is the second half of a draft of a composition. The sentences are numbered for ease of reference. Some parts of the passage need to be revised. Read the passage, then circle the letter of the best answer to each question below and write it on the blank. If the best answer is to leave a part unchanged, choose the letter for NO CHANGE.

Personal Space (continued)

[16]A bedroom is a personal space in more ways than one. [17]First, only those people we trust are welcome inside. [18]We may limit access to our bedrooms more strictly, denying access even to family members. [19]When friends of the family come visiting, we keep them in the living room, a more public space. [20]It is our one place to go to get away from everyone, and we guard it nearly as fiercely as body space.

[21]The space around our bodies is important as well. [22]It is a buffer zone that other people cannot cross without permission. [23]We meet new people. [24]We stand back a bit. [25]We may touch briefly in a handshake, but that is the extent of sharing personal space. [26]Anything more would be uncomfortable. [27]Friends are welcome to stand close, to sit shoulder-to-shoulder, and to hug us. [28]Friends can be trusted in our personal space.

[29]All these spaces—school locker, car, bedroom, and body space—are areas that we control personally. [30]What's more, we control who touches our belongings and who borrows our clothing. [31]We decide who gets in and who doesn't. [32]We protect these spaces passionately, and we depend upon them to meet our needs for comfort and privacy.

_____ **8.** What is the best sequence of sentences in the first paragraph above?

    F. NO CHANGE

    G. 16, 20, 17, 18, 19

    H. 17, 18, 19, 20, 16

    J. 16, 17, 19, 18, 20

_____ **9.** Which of the following revisions to sentence 21 is most needed?

    A. NO CHANGE

    B. Add "On the other hand," before "The space around."

    C. Change "important as well" to "the most personal of all personal spaces."

    D. Delete "as well."

_____ **10.** Which of the following revisions to sentence 25 is most needed?

    F. NO CHANGE

    G. Put a period after "handshake" and begin a new sentence with "That is."

    H. Change "but" to "and."

    J. Change "the extent of sharing personal space" to "all."

11. Which is the best revision of the underlined portion of sentence 32 (reproduced below)?

We protect these spaces passionately, and we depend upon them to meet our needs for comfort and privacy.

    A. NO CHANGE

    B. Add "In conclusion," before "We protect."

    C. Add "However," before "We protect."

    D. Add "For this reason," before "We protect."

12. Which is the best revision of the underlined portion of sentence 27 (reproduced below)?

Friends are welcome to stand close, to sit shoulder-to-shoulder, and to hug us.

    F. NO CHANGE

    G. Friends, on the other hand, are

    H. In summary, friends are

    J. Friends, for example, are

13. Which of the following revisions to sentence 23 is most needed?

    A. NO CHANGE

    B. Change the sentence to "When meeting new people," and add it to the beginning of sentence 24.

    C. Add "For example" to the beginning of sentence 23.

    D. Change the sentence to "To meet new people," and add it to the beginning of sentence 24.

14. Which of the following sentences goes off topic?

    F. sentence 32

    G. sentence 19

    H. sentence 30

    J. sentence 26

15. Which is the best change to the sequence of sentences in the second paragraph above?

    A. NO CHANGE

    B. Move sentence 28 to be the first sentence in the paragraph.

    C. Move sentences 27-28 to be before sentence 21.

    D. Move sentence 22 to be after sentence 28.

WRITING APPLICATIONS
Essay Prompts

The following assignments ask you to write complete compositions. Each one offers an opportunity for you to showcase your skills in writing and revising sentences and paragraphs. To do your best work, use the Sentence Revision Checklist on pages 203–204 and the Paragraph Revision Checklist on pages 204–205 as guides for writing and revising. In addition, your teacher may provide an essay revision checklist or may instruct you to use the checklist on page 206.

Informative Essays

Assignment A:

Some people we meet fade out of our lives, barely leaving a mark. Other people change our lives forever. Write an essay telling about one person (friend, mentor, teacher, sibling, etc.) who has changed your life in a specific way. Explain how the person caused the change, what the change was, and how your life was different. Use specific details and examples to make your points clear.

Assignment B:

A bumper sticker slogan quips, "Well-behaved women rarely make history." If you substitute "people" for "women," what does this slogan mean to you? Write an essay explaining your ideas. Develop your explanation by giving examples from your studies, experience, or observations.

Assignment C:

Suppose aliens from outer space really did exist, and they landed next to your school's football field during your homecoming game. What do you think the aliens would think of earthlings? Write an essay explaining what people's clothing, behavior, and speech suggest about what humans are like and/or what they value.

Assignment D:

Many people want to eat healthier, but they do not know how to make the switch from unhealthy to healthy eating habits. Write an essay explaining a step-by-step process that will help someone put healthy eating habits into place.

Assignment E:

Elie Wiesel, a Holocaust survivor, said this: "Wherever men or women are persecuted because of their race, religion, or politics, that place must—at that moment—become the center of the universe." Write an essay telling about one "center of the universe." For example, you could focus on an inner-city neighborhood nearby or on a faraway African country. Either way, identify the place and explain the persecution.

Assignment F:

An essay test can cause anxiety in even the best students. Many students are unsure how to prepare, and once they are writing the test, they are unsure how to use their time. Write an essay explaining techniques for preparing for and taking an essay test.

Persuasive Essays

Assignment G:

As the saying goes, money can't buy happiness. Do you agree or disagree with this claim? Write an essay to help readers see your point of view on the issue of money and happiness.

Assignment H:

Lawmakers have set minimum age requirements for voting, driving, smoking, drinking, and entering the military. Do you think lawmakers should set a minimum age requirement for getting married? Write an essay to persuade readers to agree with your point of view on this issue.

Assignment I:

As a child, Cal Ripken Jr. loved baseball, and for a class paper he wrote, "Reading is essential to become a baseball player." Do you think that being a proficient reader is essential to success in all careers, including sports, or in just some careers? Write an essay persuading readers that proficiency in reading is or is not essential to all careers.

Assignment J:

Do you think a college degree earned by taking courses over the Internet should be respected as much as a college degree earned by attending classes at a traditional campus? Write an essay explaining the reasons for your point of view.

Assignment K:

A Mexican proverb states, "A person born to be a flowerpot will not go beyond the porch." This proverb suggests that fate, or destiny, determines the course of a person's life. Do you agree or disagree with this idea? Write an essay persuading readers to accept your point of view on fate.

Assignment L:

Jane Addams, recipient of the Nobel Peace Prize, said, "Action is indeed the sole medium [method] of expression for ethics." (Ethics is concerned with distinguishing good from bad, right from wrong.) How do you think this quote applies to people your age? Write an essay persuading readers to agree with your perspective on action and ethics.

Sentence and Paragraph Composition and Revision

PART 1

Directions: The following passage is the first half of a draft of a composition. The sentences are numbered for ease of reference. Some parts of the passage need to be revised. Read the passage, then circle the letter of the best answer to each question below and write it on the blank. If the best answer is to leave a part unchanged, circle the letter for NO CHANGE.

Home, Strict Home?

1Nearly 220,000 teens responded to a 1997 survey by USA weekend magazine. **2**The subject? **3**Teens and freedom. **4**The general idea of the survey was what kinds of freedoms teens have, and another general idea was what freedoms they *wish* they had. **5**Teens spoke out on freedom in general, authority figures, and freedoms at home and school. **6**Survey results show that teens are eager to claim freedom while accepting the necessity of certain limits.

7On the subject of freedom in general, nearly half of the respondents said they do not have enough. **8**Big surprise there. **9**Teens are known for pushing the limits. **10**They edge closer to full-fledged independence. **11**It's only natural to want more freedom, including freedoms guaranteed by the Constitution, as most people of all ages would agree. **12**Only 16 percent said they have too much freedom, over a third—37 percent—said they have "the right amount of freedom."

13A teenager reports to authority figures everywhere they go. **14**Even when teens move about town, their are law enforcement officials and store security guards. **15**At home there are parents, guardians, or relatives. **16**At school, there are teachers, principals, and coaches. **17**But who is most responsible for setting restrictions on teenagers? **18**Parents are, said 44 percent of respondents.

_____ **1.** Which is the best revision of the underlined portion of sentence 1 (reproduced below)?

1Nearly 220,000 teens responded to a 1997 survey by <u>USA weekend</u> magazine.

   A. NO CHANGE

   B. "USA Weekend"

   C. <u>USA Weekend</u>

   D. <u>USA weekend</u>

2. Which of the following is the best revision of sentence 4?

   F. NO CHANGE

   G. What kinds of freedoms do teens have, and what freedoms do they *wish* they had?

   H. The general idea of the survey was freedoms.

   J. The survey was about what kinds of freedoms teens have, and it was also about what freedoms they *wish* they had.

3. Which of the following is the best revision of sentence 6?

   A. NO CHANGE

   B. Survey results show that teens are eager to claim freedom.

   C. Survey results show that teens accept freedom and limits.

   D. Survey results show that teens are eager to claim freedom in most areas of their lives including home and school, and they also accept the necessity of certain limits in certain areas.

4. Which of the following revisions to sentence 10 is most needed?

   F. NO CHANGE

   G. Delete sentence 10 since it is off topic.

   H. Change sentence 10 to a participial phrase ("Edging closer to independence") and put it at the beginning of sentence 9.

   J. Add a comma after "independence" and use "and" to join sentence 10 and sentence 11.

5. Which is the best revision of the underlined portion of sentence 12 (reproduced below)?

   Only 16 percent said they have too much <u>freedom, over</u> a third—37 percent— said they have "the right amount of freedom."

   A. NO CHANGE

   B. freedom; in fact, over

   C. freedom, while over

   D. freedom over

6. Which sentence in the second paragraph goes off topic?

   F. NO CHANGE

   G. 9

   H. 11

   J. 12

_____ **7.** Which is the best revision of the underlined portion of sentence 13 (reproduced below)?

A teenager reports to authority figures everywhere <u>they go</u>.

A. NO CHANGE

B. he or she goes

C. they goes

D. it goes

_____ **8.** In the third paragraph, which sequence of sentences best follows sentence 13?

F. NO CHANGE

G. 15, 16, 14, 17, 18

H. 17, 18, 14, 15, 16

J. 14, 17, 18, 15, 16

_____ **9.** Which word in sentence 14 is misspelled?

A. NO CHANGE

B. enforcement

C. security

D. their

_____ **10.** Which is the best revision of the underlined portion of sentence 18 (reproduced below)?

Parents are, <u>said</u> 44 percent of respondents.

F. NO CHANGE

G. say

H. says

J. has said

PART 2

Directions: The following passage is the second half of a draft of a composition. The sentences are numbered for ease of reference. Some parts of the passage need to be revised. Read the passage and circle the letter of the best answer to each question below. If the best answer is to leave a part unchanged, circle the letter for NO CHANGE.

Home, Strict Home? (continued)

[19]What about freedoms at home? In some areas, teens have plenty. [20]Most said they can choose their own music, select their own friends, and money spent however they want.

[21]Teens are vigilant against too much restriction. [22]Just over two-thirds oppose putting a chip in the television to block certain shows. [23]Seventy percent said there should be no restrictions on a teenagers Internet usage. [24]Installing a computer program to limit Internet access, nearly two-thirds oppose this.

25Teenagers want their freedom at school, too. **26**Drugs and weapons pose safety hazards. **27**However, barely more than half (58 percent) of respondents think its okay for their lockers to be searched for these items without permission. **28**Three-fourths said yes to banning clothes with gang symbols from school.

29When it comes to clothing, students want their freedom, to a point. **30**At least 80 percent believe that baggy clothing, hats, cut-off pants, and earrings on boys should be allowed. **31**Thirty-five percent think short skirts on girls should be banned, and 42 percent think exposed midriffs should be banned.

32In the end, most teenagers—and adults, for that matter—walk a fine line. **33**On one side is the protection and security of rules and limitations. **34**Then there is great, glorious freedom, with all its risks and rewards. **35**Exactly *how* to walk this line is each person's personal decision.

_____ **11.** Which is the best revision of the underlined portion of sentence 20 (reproduced below)?

Most said they can choose their own music, select their own friends, and <u>money spent however they want</u>.

A. NO CHANGE

B. spend money however they want

C. money spent however

D. spending money however they want

_____ **12.** Which is the best revision of the underlined portion of sentence 21 (reproduced below)?

<u>Teens are</u> vigilant against too much restriction.

F. NO CHANGE

G. Elsewhere, teens are

H. In other areas at home, teens are

J. Similarly, teens are

_____ **13.** Which of the following revisions to sentence 22 is most needed?

A. NO CHANGE

B. Move "to block certain shows" to be before "Just."

C. Change "putting" to "to put."

D. Add a comma after "shows" to join sentence 22 to sentence 23.

_____ **14.** Which of the following revisions to sentence 23 is most needed?

F. NO CHANGE

G. Change "restrictions" to "restriction's."

H. Change "there" to "they're."

J. Change "teenagers" to "teenager's."

_____ **15.** Which of the following is the best revision of sentence 24?

    A. NO CHANGE

    B. Nearly two-thirds oppose installing a computer program to limit Internet access.

    C. Installing a computer program to limit Internet access. Nearly two-thirds oppose this.

    D. There is a computer program that nearly two-thirds oppose that limits Internet access.

_____ **16.** Which of the following is the best revision of sentence 25?

    F. NO CHANGE

    G. Teenagers want their freedom at school, too, because the line between freedom and safety is difficult to draw.

    H. Teenagers want their freedom at school, too, but the line between freedom and safety is difficult to draw.

    J. Teenagers want their freedom at school, too, in addition to wanting freedom to dress as they choose.

_____ **17.** Which of the following revisions to sentence 27 is most needed?

    A. NO CHANGE

    B. Change "its" to "it's."

    C. Change "barely" to "barly."

    D. Change "half" to "halve."

_____ **18.** Which of the following revisions to sentence 28 is most needed?

    F. NO CHANGE

    G. Move sentence 28 to be after sentence 31, in the next paragraph.

    H. Put quotation marks around "yes."

    J. Delete "from school."

_____ **19.** Which is the best revision of the underlined portion of sentence 31 (reproduced below)?

Thirty-five percent think short skirts on girls should be banned, and 42 percent think exposed midriffs should be banned.

    A. NO CHANGE

    B. Obviously, thirty-five percent

    C. In particular, thirty-five percent

    D. In contrast, thirty-five percent

_____ **20.** Which is the best revision of the underlined portion of sentence 34 (reproduced below)?

<u>Then there</u> is great, glorious freedom, with all its risks and rewards.

   F. NO CHANGE

   G. Finally, there is

   H. There is

   J. On the other side is

Editing Checklists

Sentence Revision Checklist

Use this checklist as a guide when you write and revise sentences. It includes the characteristics of strong sentences (taught in Lessons 1–4) and problem areas in grammar and composition (taught in Lessons 5–8).

STYLE

Make sure your sentences are strong and forceful by including these stylistic qualities:

_____ conciseness

_____ clarity and specificity

_____ unity

_____ active voice unless there is a specific reason for passive voice

_____ sentence variety in length and structure

GRAMMAR

Proofread your sentences to correct grammar errors.

_____ sentence fragment

_____ run-on sentence

_____ comma splice

_____ incorrect verb form

_____ lack of agreement between subject and verb

_____ inconsistent verb tense

_____ incorrect form of modifier (adverbs and adjectives)

_____ misplaced modifier

_____ dangling modifier

_____ lack of agreement between pronoun and antecedent

_____ pronoun with no clear antecedent

_____ double negative

Proofread your sentences to correct errors in mechanics.

_____ missing or misused comma (**,**)

_____ missing or misused semicolon (**;**)

_____ missing or misused colon (**:**)

_____ missing or misused apostrophe (**'**)

_____ missing quotation marks around direct quote (" . . . ")

_____ missing quotation marks around title of short work (" . . . ")

_____ missing *italics* or <u>underlining</u> for title of longer work

_____ missing or misused capital letter

_____ misspelled word

_____ misspelled plural of a noun

Paragraph Revision Checklist

Use this checklist as a guide when you write and revise paragraphs. It includes the characteristics of strong paragraphs (taught in Lessons 9–16) and techniques for revising paragraphs to make them stronger (taught in Lessons 17–21).

WRITING PARAGRAPHS

Make sure paragraphs are strong and unified by including these qualities:

All Paragraphs:

_____ appropriate length

_____ unity

_____ topic sentence (in body paragraphs)

_____ well-developed reasons or examples that support the topic sentence, arranged in a logical sequence

_____ clincher sentence, if appropriate

Introductory Paragraph:

_____ identification of the composition's topic

_____ narrowing of the topic to one specific idea

_____ expression of the main idea in a thesis

Conclusion Paragraph:

_____ restatement of the thesis

_____ summary of key ideas

_____ final emphasis on value of composition's content

REVISING THE TOPIC SENTENCE

Revise topic sentences to make sure they are

_____ specific, not vague

_____ focused, not broad

_____ in agreement with supporting sentences, not off topic

REVISING FOR UNITY

Revise paragraphs to correct the following errors:

_____ sentences off topic

_____ more than one main idea

_____ unclear transitions

_____ unclear or illogical relationships between ideas

ARRANGING THE ORDER OF SENTENCES

Revise the order of sentences in a paragraph by

_____ arranging reasons to build up to the strongest

_____ arranging examples to build up to the most important

_____ arranging examples related to a time sequence in chronological order

_____ arranging examples of steps in a process in order from first to last

_____ in comparisons, arranging like qualities together and unlike qualities together

ADDING SENTENCE VARIETY

Add sentence variety in a paragraph by

_____ varying sentence types (simple, compound, complex, compound-complex)

_____ varying sentence lengths

_____ including an occasional question, exclamation, or command/polite request, when appropriate

_____ varying sentence beginnings

_____ using appositives

_____ using verbals (participles, infinitives, gerunds)

Essay Revision Checklist

Use this checklist in conjunction with the Sentence and Paragraph Revision Checklists when you write and revise compositions.

_____ Does the essay have an *introduction paragraph* that introduces the topic, narrows down the topic, and states the thesis?

_____ Does the essay have a *thesis* that states a specific point of view about the topic? The *thesis* should be meaty enough to require explanation or proof in several body paragraphs.

_____ Does each *body paragraph* include a topic sentence, if necessary?

_____ Does each *body paragraph* clearly explain or prove an aspect of the thesis (stated in the topic sentence)?

_____ Are the *body paragraphs* arranged in a clear and logical order?

_____ Do *transitions* help readers move from idea to idea and from paragraph to paragraph?

_____ Does the essay use *correct grammar*?

_____ Does the essay use *correct punctuation*?

_____ Does the essay use *correct capitalization*?

_____ Does the essay use *correct spelling*?

_____ Does the paragraph have a *conclusion paragraph* that restates the main idea, sums up the main points, and emphasizes the value of the writer's point of view?

Glossary

active voice	In a sentence written in active voice, the subject performs the action of the verb.
clause	A related sequence of words that has a subject and its verb. A *main clause* expresses a complete idea and can stand alone as a sentence. A *subordinate clause* does not express a complete idea and cannot stand alone as a sentence.
clincher sentence	Drives home the point that the paragraph is making.
comma splice	Two or more sentences joined with only a comma.
complex sentence	A sentence containing one main clause and at least one subordinate clause.
compound sentence	A sentence containing two or more main clauses and no subordinate clauses.
compound-complex sentence	A sentence containing at least two main clauses and at least one subordinate clause.
conclusion paragraph	Usually the last paragraph of a composition; it drives home the composition's main idea.
fragment	A word group punctuated as a sentence yet lacking a subject, a verb, or both.
gerund	A verb form used as a noun in a sentence. A gerund ends in *ing*. A *gerund phrase* includes a gerund and any objects and modifiers.
infinitive	A verb form that can be used as a noun, an adjective, or an adverb. Most infinitives begin with *to,* as in *to forgive*. An *infinitive phrase* includes an infinitive and any objects and modifiers.
introduction paragraph	Usually the first paragraph of a composition; it introduces the paper's topic, states the paper's thesis, and identifies the paper's main points.
paragraph	A group of sentences telling about one topic.
participle	A verb form that may be used as part of a verb phrase or as an adjective. A *participial phrase* includes a participle and any objects and modifiers.
passive voice	In a sentence written in passive voice, the subject is acted upon; it receives the action of the verb.
run-on	Two or more sentences run together without punctuation or a conjunction between them.

simple sentence   A sentence containing one subject and one verb (one main clause).

thesis sentence   States the main idea of a composition.

topic sentence   States the topic, or main idea, of a paragraph.

verbal   A verb form that is not used as a verb, but rather as a noun, an adjective, or an adverb.

Index

M

Main clauses, 2
  in complex sentences, 4, 14
  in compound-complex sentences, 4, 14
  in compound sentences, 4
  in simple sentences, 4
Main ideas
  identifying in introductory paragraphs, 133
  relating all sentence parts to, 26–27
Mechanics, errors in, 78–79
Modifiers, 71–74. *See also* Adjectives; Adverbs
  correct form of, 71–72
  dangling, 73
  piled-up, 22
  placement of, 72

N

Names, capitalization of words used as, 81
Negatives, avoiding double, 77
Nonessential clauses, 8, 9
Noun(s)
  proper, 81
  spelling plurals of, 84
Noun clauses, words that introduce, 8
Numbers, spelling out, 87

O

Organizational methods
  chronological, 123
  compare and contrast, 123
  increasing importance, 123
  sequence, 123

P

Paragraph(s)
  arranging, in a composition, 144–145
  clincher sentence in, 115–118
  conclusion, 141–143
  defined, 102
  developing with examples, 119–126
  developing with reasons, 127–132
  elements of strong, 146
  indentation of first line, 102
  informative, 119–126
  introductory, 133–135
  length of, 103
  order of sentences in, 175–178
  persuasive, 127–132
  sentence variety in, 179–182
  topic sentence in, 111–114, 162–170
  unity in, 105–110, 171–174
Paragraph revision, 161–188
  checklist for, 187–188, 204–205
  order of sentences in, 175–178
  sentence variety in, 179–182
  topic sentences in, 162–170
  for unity, 171–174
Parallel structure, 28
Participial phrase, 40
Participle, 37

past, 66
Passive voice, 30–31
Past participle, 66, 68
Past tense, 66, 68
Personal titles, abbreviations for, 87
Persuasive paragraphs, 127–132
  topic sentence for, 127–132
Phrases, 37
  verbal, 40
Piled-up modifiers, 22
Place, transition words and phrases in showing, 109
Plurals, spelling, for nouns, 84
Possessives, apostrophe in forming, 79
Prefixes, spelling rules for adding, 82
Prepositions, ending sentence with, 76
principal, principle, 86
Pronouns
  agreement with antecedent, 74–75
  indefinite, 68–69
Proper adjectives, capitalization of, 81
Proper nouns, capitalization of, 81

Q

Quotation marks
  to enclose direct quotations, 79
  to enclose titles of short works, 79

R

Reasons, developing paragraphs with, 127–132
Regions, capitalization of names of specific, 81
Relative pronouns, to introduce adjective clauses, 8
Run-on sentences, 60–62

S

Salutation, capitalization of first word and nouns in, 81
Semicolons
  in correcting comma splices, 63
  in correcting run-on sentences, 60
  in forming compound sentences, 4, 7
  to join items in series, 78
  to join sentences, 78
Sentence(s)
  active voice, 30–31
  capitalization of first word in, 81
  clauses in, 2
  clincher, 115–118
  complex, 2, 4, 14, 43
  compound, 2, 4, 43
  compound-complex, 2, 4, 14, 15, 43
  conciseness in, 17–23
  ending with proposition, 76
  forming complete, 2
  grammar errors in, 66–77
  length and purpose of, 35–36
  passive voice, 30–31
  run-on, 60–61
  simple, 2, 3, 4, 5, 43
  structure of, 37, 39, 40
  topic, 111–114
  types of, 2

unity in, 26–34
  variety of, in paragraphs, 179–182
Sentence fragments, 2, 56, 58
Sentence revision, 5, 17, 55–92
  avoiding series of *that, which,* or *who* clauses, 27–28
  checklist for, 91–92, 203–204
  comma splices in, 62–63
  fragments in, 56, 58
  grammar errors in, 66–77
  mechanics errors in, 78–79
  order of sentence in paragraphs, 175–178
  run-on sentences, 60–61
Sequence, arranging examples in, 123
Series
  commas in forming, 78
  semicolons in forming, 78
Sexist language, 75
Simple sentences, 2, 3, 4, 5, 43
since, 12
so, 12
Specificity, 23–25
Spelling
  abbreviations, 87
  adding prefixes, 82
  adding suffix *ly* or *ness,* 82
  doubling final consonant, 83
  final *e* before consonant, 83
  final *e* before vowel, 83
  final *y* preceded by consonant, 83
  i before *e,* 82
  numbers, 87
  plurals of nouns, 84
Subject-verb agreement, 68–69
Subordinate clauses, 2, 8
  in complex sentences, 4, 14
  in compound-complex sentences, 4, 14
  essential versus nonessential, 8, 9
  problem of multiple, 9
  revising, to form complete sentence, 58–59
  subject and verb in, 58
  words that introduce, 8
Subordinating conjunctions, 11, 24
  in correcting comma splices, 63
  to introduce adverb clauses, 8
  relationships shown by, 12
Suffixes, spelling rules for adding, 82
Summarization, transition words and phrases in showing, 109

T

than, 12
than, then, 86
That clauses, avoiding series of, 27–28
their, there, they're, 86
there, they're, their, 86
Thesis
  identifying in introductory paragraphs, 133, 134
  steps in writing strong, 135–136
they're, their, there, 86
Time, transition words and phrases in showing sequence of, 109